NLP coaching

Coaching in Practice series

The aim of this series is to help coaching professionals gain a broader understanding of the challenges and issues they face in coaching, enabling them to make the leap from being a 'good enough' coach to an outstanding one. This series is an essential aid for both the novice coach eager to learn how to grow a coaching practice, and the more experienced coach looking for new knowledge and strategies. Combining theory with practice, it provides a comprehensive guide to becoming successful in this rapidly expanding profession.

Published and forthcoming titles:
Bluckert, P., *Psychological Dimensions of Executive Coaching* (2006)
Hay, J., *Reflective Practice and Supervision for Coaches* (2007)
Rogers, J., *Developing a Coaching Business* (2006)
Vaughan Smith, J., *Therapist into Coach* (2006)

NLP coaching

Phil Hayes

Open University Press

Open University Press
McGraw-Hill Education
McGraw-Hill House
Shoppenhangers Road
Maidenhead
Berkshire
England
SL6 2QL

email: enquiries@openup.co.uk
world wide web: www.openup.co.uk

and Two Penn Plaza, New York, NY 10121–2289, USA

First published 2006

A catalogue record of this book is available from the British Library

ISBN-10: 0335 220 592 (pb) 0335 220 606 (hb)
ISBN-13: 978 0335 220 595 (pb) 978 0335 220 601 (hb)

Library of Congress Cataloging-in-Publication Data
CIP data applied for

Typeset by YHT Ltd, London
Printed in Poland by OZ Graf. S.A.
www.polskabook.pl

The *McGraw·Hill* Companies

Contents

For Mandy, Max and Flora

Series editor's preface

The coaching world is expanding. A profession that was largely unknown a decade ago is now an attractive second career for increasing numbers of people looking for new ways of growing their interest in the development of people. Some observers estimate that the number of new coaches joining the market is doubling every year.

Yet while there are many books that cater for the beginner coach, including my own book, also published by Open University Press, *Coaching Skills: A Handbook*, there are relatively few that explore and deepen more specialist aspects of the role. That is the purpose of this series. It is called *Coaching in Practice* because the aim is to unite theory and practice in an accessible way. The books are short, designed to be easily understood without in any way compromising on the integrity of the ideas they explore. All are written by senior coaches with, in every case, many years of hands-on experience.

This series is for you if you are undertaking or completing your coaching training and are perhaps in the early stages of the unpredictability, pleasures and dilemmas that working with actual clients brings. Now that you have passed the honeymoon stage, you may have begun to notice the limitations of your approaches and knowledge. You are eager for more information and guidance. You probably know that it is hard to make the leap between being a good-enough coach and an outstanding one. You are thirsty for more help and challenge. You may also be one of the many people still contemplating a career in coaching. If so, these books will give you useful direction on many of the issues that preoccupy, perplex and delight the working coach. That is where I hope you will find the *Coaching in Practice* series so useful.

NLP (Neuro-Linguistic Programming) has been around for many years and is a rich source of inspiration for any coach. But how exactly do you make best use of its many ideas when you are a practising coach? How do you avoid the sense that NLP is just a set of techniques looking for a problem? This intensely practical book is written by one of the most experienced and successful executive coaches in the UK and his book will show you how to weave NLP seamlessly into the very best of coaching practice in a way that goes beyond 'technique' and into the heart of the coach–client relationship.

Jenny Rogers, Series Editor

Acknowledgements

I heap huge showers of thanks and praise on Jenny Rogers for her wise and patient editing of this book. Working with Jenny has been a wonderful learning experience for the past sixteen years, and once again she has shown me how something really ought to be done.

I would also like to thank all my colleagues at Management Futures Ltd for their coaching wisdom, and for providing the rich backdrop of comradeship and professionalism that forms a major part of the context for this book.

Many thanks to Stephen Waters for doing the pictures.

1   Neuro-Linguistic Programming, coaching and me
It's getting harder to see the join

Aims of the book

In the early 1990s I was working as a senior consultant in the BBC's management training department. At the time John Birt was in charge, and was systematically requiring departments such as ours to charge for their services and act as internal trading units. Business was good, but we noticed that it was hard to attract the most senior managers to our courses. However, quite quickly we also noticed that a significant number of these senior figures, while unwilling to register on the courses, were quite eager to arrange one-to-one sessions to discuss their management and leadership issues in a confidential environment. The great thing was that these senior managers seemed to benefit directly from the sessions: there were clear practical spin-offs as well as learning. Coaching worked, and was seen to work, with people who previously had wanted little or nothing to do with professional development. Gradually our one-to-one sessions evolved into a more formal and conscious coaching offer. The style we developed grew first in that department, then in the context of the developing methodologies and ethos of Management Futures Ltd, the company where I am now a director. My own style of coaching has always had a strong Neuro-Linguistic Programming (NLP) accent and this influence has found its way into the Management Futures approach.

This book is probably for you if . . .

- you are already coaching, or learning to coach, and want to expand your repertoire of skills and expertise by learning something of the practical applications of NLP in a coaching context
- you are an NLP practitioner who wants to learn more about coaching in general and also how your NLP skills might apply in a coaching context
- you are a manager trained in coaching and want to build your coaching repertoire.

The main aim of the book is to look at the *practical* applications of NLP in typical business-based coaching situations. Most of the book describes real-life coaching situations and how NLP has helped to enrich the coaching process. Most of the material here could fairly be described as 'first-generation' NLP, consisting mainly of robust, tried-and-tested material.

There are detailed descriptions and systematic instructions where appropriate. However, this book does not attempt to describe the whole of NLP in a definitive way – there are numerous other books that do this and references to some of them are included. I try to offer a degree of *depth* of description of the use of specific techniques that is generally not available from the standard NLP texts, and a depth of experience in their practical application, including potential pitfalls in their use. I do not claim the NLP techniques described here to be in any way purist descriptions: I have been using NLP in coaching for a long time and have developed, in conjunction with my colleagues, a number of little tweaks and variations that have made the NLP material really come alive in a coaching context. I have also noticed that the responses that clients have to the techniques vary so widely that the bullet-point approach to describing the techniques found in many NLP books just do not prepare you adequately for their use in real-life coaching scenarios.

There is something of a permeable membrane between NLP and the rest of the development world – NLP has modelled and adapted approaches from many other sources and I do not find it useful to be too fussy about distinctions between what 'is' and what 'is not' NLP. A practical way of thinking about this book is that it is about business coaching with an NLP accent. In reality I use plenty of other coaching techniques as well as the NLP techniques I describe here, and share the fundamentals of the approach described by my colleague Jenny Rogers in her book *Coaching Skills: A Handbook*.

NLP is advancing in its sophistication. Some of the techniques and approaches that NLP is spawning are highly sophisticated and elaborate. There is, however, a danger of too much esotericism alongside this sophistication, at least as far as many coaching clients are concerned. This book focuses primarily on the foundation material taught on NLP practitioner courses – a really outstanding body of material.

I have found over the years that when NLP is effective in coaching its usefulness manifests itself in two main dimensions. One of these is inside the coach's head – their underpinning attitudes and presuppositions about NLP as a search for excellence and resourcefulness in self and others. The second dimension is a set of NLP-derived tools and approaches that are direct and simple enough for the business client to take on board without fear of alienating them. The very term 'NLP' can be off-putting for a large proportion of business clients, many of whom are fearful of, and sceptical about, anything that might smack, according to their world view, of 'psycho-babble'. One has to remember that many business clients in particular come to coaching having had little exposure to modern development techniques. This is truer in some sectors than others of course. I recently worked with a senior military officer and I introduced the subject of rapport skills: his blank look told me I needed metaphorically to turn back a few pages and check his understanding of the concept of rapport. In his effort to build understanding he offered the information that, while he had no strong idea about whether his own rapport skills were up to scratch, he at least had not shot anyone for several months. I think he might have been joking.

I tend to use an NLP approach and work with NLP techniques without direct reference to NLP at all – I rarely label the techniques I use in coaching. The majority of the approaches described in this book are those I have found it easy to introduce to a client while maintaining a rapport – a reflection and recognition of *their* world view, and *their* starting point in coaching rather than mine. There are numerous occasions when the more sophisticated techniques are extremely useful in coaching – the key is to use the techniques in a manner that ensures the maintenance of rapport, and sometimes it takes time to build the confidence of the client in both you as a coach and the NLP tool-box.

This book is emphatically not about techniques in search of problems to solve. Rather it is about looking at some of the real scenarios and issues that typically occur in coaching and showing how NLP approaches can assist in the coaching process.

So this book might *not* be for you if you want a definitive NLP textbook, or a definitive coaching guide – I assume at least a basic knowledge of coaching. I would also suggest you look elsewhere if you want to read about academic research into either coaching or NLP, or if you want to engage further in the many debates about coaching and its relationship to other approaches and disciplines such as therapy.

However, I hope you will think of the book as an interesting companion and practical guide to a significant part of the territory of coaching, written by a practitioner who has taken a long, and sometimes stumbling, path to a particular version of expertise and experience. I also hope you will experience some of the excitement and privilege I have felt at helping some wonderfully resourceful clients to make progress.

What is coaching?

Coaching is getting bigger all the time. A recent CIPD (Chartered Institute of Personnel and Development) study suggests that something like 85 per cent of organizations in the UK employ some kind of coaching as a means of developing effectiveness in their staff. Ten years ago coaching was virtually unknown as a business tool in the UK. To some degree the growth of the profession can be seen as paralleled by the growth in awareness of the whole subject of *emotional intelligence*. Emotional intelligence (or EI) is based on the recognition that personal effectiveness, and career success, is based only to a limited degree on IQ. Instead, more and more research is saying that career success is dependent upon the ability to understand oneself, to manage oneself effectively, to understand others and to manage relationships. In practical terms, this means things like managing your own motivation and stress, being able to negotiate and influence effectively, build and lead teams, manage your relationship with your boss, and so on.

These were subjects previously thought of as 'soft' skills, the implication sometimes being that they were almost a sign of soft*ness*. In today's business world, formal qualifications, technical skills and formal knowledge are just commodities – everyone expects a degree of competence as a given. You may get appointed and achieve initial career development on the back of your IQ and/or your qualifications, but ultimately a lack of EI will potentially limit or derail your career.

Coaching sits as one of the most effective ways in which people at work can build their EI, putting them in a position where they can maximize their career potential and utilize all of their personal resources in reaching their goals.

Additionally, an increasing number of managers and leaders in organizational life are discovering that by learning coaching skills for themselves they can have a direct impact on the effectiveness of their staff and in helping their staff to build EI themselves – it is a generative process. This can, and does, have a direct effect on the bottom-line effectiveness of individual organizations.

However, coaching is more than about developing EI, important though this is. Coaching is also about helping clients to plan careers, dream, deal with crises, refocus their lives, create a sense of meaning and belief for themselves and generally refresh the way they work and lead their lives. It is catalytic in effect and, at its best, transformational for the whole person.

The key to all this is that coaching actually works. I have been engaged in personal, team and organizational development activities of varying sorts for nearly thirty years and have seen nothing like it for far-reaching and cost-effective results.

Defining coaching

For all its dynamic achievement, growing profile and potential, coaching in a business context can be difficult to define, even for coaches. An illustration: our company, Management Futures Ltd, runs a five-day coaching skills course, and as part of the course we ask participants to arrange a practice telephone coaching exercise on the evening of the second day. As part of the preparation for this task, we ask participants to write down their answer to the question 'What is coaching?' in no more than a sentence. We then get them to stand up and mingle together, as if at a party, and take it in turns to ask, and then answer, this apparently simple question, assuming no prior knowledge on the part of the person who is doing the asking. At the end of the exercise, we invite each participant to redraft their original answer in the light of having listened to the answers of their colleagues. The overall aim is that they each have at their fingertips a working definition or at least a clear description of coaching with which they can feel comfortable. Course participants usually see this as a tough exercise, because conveying a handy definition to a layperson is challenging.

It can be difficult to tie coaching down to a satisfactorily tight definition for a number of reasons:

- The term 'coach' has been synonymous with *sport* for many years. Even within sport, there have been many shades of meaning. Perhaps the most persistent and traditional image is of the track-suited, bellowing male who 'coaches' using an unsubtle concoction of exhortation and threats. In more recent years the image of the sports coach has evolved considerably, in many cases into a Svengali-like figure, a psychologically inclined 'guru' who harnesses mysterious mental techniques aimed at improving confidence, removing fear and tension, and visualizing successful outcomes. Perhaps the most noteworthy influence on coaching from the world of sport is the *Inner Game* books of Timothy Gallwey. First published in the 1970s and updated now, these books pioneered an approach to sporting excellence based on the realization that focusing on a sportsperson's personal mindset and resourcefulness was more effective than trying to teach or impose a model from the outside.
- There is confusion over the similarities with other approaches such as *mentoring, psychotherapy* and *counselling*. This issue in particular attracts a lot of debate, and indeed anxiety, among both teachers and students of coaching. I do not propose to add to the debate here except to say that I do not believe it to be *definitively* resolvable, and from the purely practical perspective I am not sure it matters that much. There is no doubt that there are overlaps between each of these disciplines – superficially they even *look* and *sound* much the same, with two people sitting in a room discussing the issues of one of them. There is also no doubt that within each of them there are great variations of approach from practitioner to practitioner and from school of thought to school of thought. Psychotherapy, for example, has within it numerous different 'orders' rather in the way that there are different sorts of monk, all trying to find God in their various ways.

In any case, coaching certainly borrows and adapts from numerous other disciplines. One of the things that seems to differentiate the really polished coach from the 'just trained' coach is a deep underlying knowledge of various other underpinning psychological theories and techniques. These include Gestalt, Psychodynamics, Transactional Analysis, Person-Centred Counselling and (of course) NLP.

So the real differences are blurred and there are numerous paradoxes at play. Within all of this, I think it fairly safe to say there are some worthwhile broad *emphases* with each of the disciplines mentioned.

- *Mentoring* is generally regarded as a relationship in which an older, wiser, more experienced person guides another, usually in a context where the mentor has a considerable degree of subject or context knowledge.
- *Psychotherapy* is usually seen as addressing psychological issues involving emotional suffering or discomfort, but there is no doubt that in some cases it can also be highly aspirational and developmental in style.
- *Counselling* is usually seen as a relationship based around a short-term issue or crisis, such as marriage guidance, trauma counselling or illness. However, there are some forms of counselling that resemble quite closely some parts of coaching, and I would repeat that there are some very blurred distinctions at times.

Coaching itself seems to have many sub-divisions, e.g. executive coaching, business coaching, life coaching, career coaching and, of course, sports coaching. The reality here is that there is likely to be far more similarity than difference in approach between these forms of coaching, and that the distinctions in name arise largely from context rather than from approach.

My own 'dinner party' definition of coaching owes a huge debt to long-time colleague and distinguished author Jenny Rogers, and to my other colleagues at Management Futures Ltd, as well as to various other writers, teachers, trainers, students and speakers I have encountered over the years. It is this:

> The coach helps the client increase their effectiveness in areas of life and work *chosen* by themselves, to goals and standards *defined* by them.

This does not always mean the client has to leave coaching groaning under the weight of an onerous action plan. Change can be achieved at the thinking and feeling levels as well as at the level of behaviour. I rather liked the definition of coaching offered by one of our students in the 'What is coaching?'

exercise described above: she said, 'Coaching is about taking someone's thinking where it has never gone before.' If someone is relieved of a burden of worry by changing the way they think about something, for example, then the principle holds good. However, it would be true to say that for the majority of clients some action will take place in their lives and work because of coaching. If nothing seems to be changing then perhaps they do not really want a coach, or they need a different coach from you.

Process not content

One of the features that underpins both coaching and NLP (and therefore makes coaching *using* NLP so powerful) is the focus that the coach has on the *process* rather than the *content*. This means in essence that the coach is concentrating on *how* a client is thinking, feeling and behaving rather than on the *what* of the issue they are working on.

There is a good analogy here with group facilitation, in which the facilitator focuses their energy on what is going on between the group members rather than on what they are actually discussing. I can remember clearly how anxious I felt about this issue in my early days as a facilitator and then as a tyro coach. As a facilitator I felt sure I would lack credibility if I did not know enough about the subject under discussion – surely the group would expect me to be an expert? My anxiety about this was nailed for ever about fourteen years ago when I facilitated an event for a very technical part of the BBC: I can honestly say I had virtually no clue what the group were talking about for most of the day. As a facilitator I focused on managing their energy and drawing to their attention any patterns of interaction that seemed unhelpful: crucially I got them through their hugely complex agenda *on time*. The day was pronounced a success by the group and the message finally got home to me: facilitation is *only about the process*.

I experienced similar anxieties in my early days as a coach. My clients seemed important and knowledgeable and I was often worried that they would consider me lacking in credibility if I was not at least respectably knowledgeable in their world of work. I assumed they would value me only for my subject expertise and advice. Gradually, though, the realization dawned that *the less I knew about the specifics of their job the better I would work with them*. This realization totally freed me up to do what I do best – to listen attentively, spot patterns of thought and feeling, and help the clients to focus in on their own resources. So, do not read on until you have repeated this to yourself several times:

Coaching is about the process, not the content.

Coaching is never about advice

The realizations I had about working on process rather than content *all the time* in coaching also freed me from the temptation to offer advice. This is often one of the hardest things new coaches find about learning to coach. After all, it feels a perfectly natural and indeed a desirable thing to do – surely your client expects it, too? The key point here is that in the end the client has to live with the changes they make – and deep down they always know what is best for them, better than does the coach (if the coach is doing the job right, i.e. getting them in touch with their personal resources). Also, if the advice goes wrong for the client, guess who (rightly) gets the blame?

Try this experiment for yourself some time: ask a friend to name something about themselves they would like to change (typical subjects are lifestyle issues such as smoking, diet, drinking and exercise, managing a troublesome relationship, taking up a new hobby, etc.). Ask them to state the issue clearly, then offer them *every piece of information and advice you have for them on the subject*. When you finish, ask them what was new for them, what they learned, and how motivated and empowered they are to make a change on the basis of your advice. The chances are strong that they will learn very little or nothing new, and that they will feel, if anything, even less inclined to make a change. You might also try asking others for all their advice and see how little positive effect it has on you.

Why do clients seek coaching?

There are many reasons for this, typically including the following:

- career development dilemmas
- relationship issues at work, e.g. managing the boss
- work/life balance issues
- issues around confidence in presenting and handling oneself, e.g. at meetings or presentations
- handling stress or dissatisfaction
- making tough and important decisions
- reality checking, e.g. are they doing the right things as a leader?

Sometimes there is a mixture of these and other issues. As to why they choose coaching as opposed to other helping techniques, I believe the answer to be in coaching's effectiveness, its growing reputation and image, and its clear personal focus.

Training, for example, can offer diminishing returns as you rise up the corporate ladder – each course seems to have less in it that directly relates to what you need to deal with. As a trainer myself, I have also noticed that more senior people can be reluctant to admit they need to improve on anything, or to expose any of their own learning needs within a group. In a confidential coaching session they can open up much more and work a lot more frankly on the issues on which they need to make progress.

They can also get a level of feedback from their coach they might never get anywhere else. It truly can be lonely at the top, and the 'blind spot' of self-knowledge that an individual executive might have about how they present to others might go unremarked *to them* for years while systematically, and unknown to them, having a negative effect on their reputation.

Counselling and psychotherapy tend primarily to deal with the emotional aspects of an issue, whereas coaching, while it often enters into these areas, is fundamentally practical in focus, leading to decisions, actions and forward plans on very tangible issues: there is little chance of psychotherapy offering much practical support to an emotionally stable and happy manager who wants to think through a strategic planning issue, for example.

The clear parallel that coaching *does* have with counselling is in its personal focus – the level of attention paid to the client's own personal agenda and to themselves as human beings. Many senior leaders often lack a trustworthy, discreet and helpful equal partner they can confide in and work issues through with – and this is where coaching offers a uniquely focused service.

Coaching does *not* foster dependency. Coaching contracts are generally short – say four to six two-hour sessions – and very focused as a result. The aim is to work with a degree of focused rigour in helping a client to make progress on their agenda of the day.

How a coaching session works

There is probably no such thing as a 'typical' session, but the majority of sessions I and my colleagues hold will be two hours long, and generally a client will take up between four and six of these spread over several months. Wherever possible the sessions take place at our office premises, where we have purpose-built rooms, or in hired office space such as that offered by companies such as Regus. In any case we strongly encourage clients not to use their own offices – there is just no way in which they can mentally detach from the direct pressures of work on their own premises, and the risk of interruption is too great. On the two or three occasions I have been talked into coaching on the client's premises the sessions have not worked well – the feared interruptions have invariably happened and the clients have been clearly distracted. Many clients have also reported the benefits of having a short journey to their coaching session – it allows them to clear their thoughts in preparation and to digest their thoughts afterwards.

Bearing in mind that there are *many* variations, a first session will usually include the following, in this approximate order:

- rapport-building
- contracting/creating a working partnership
- background information/brief autobiography
- exploration of issue(s) to be discussed
- exploring the significance of the issues
- exploring motivation and energy to tackle the issue/issues
- exploring options for change and/or blockages to progress
- identification of possible ways forward
- exploring the feasibility and potential outcomes of these possible ways forward
- planning to deal with any potential self-sabotage
- committing to actions or next steps as appropriate
- exploring issues of accountability
- feedback to the coach.

Second and subsequent sessions will feature a review of what has happened between sessions, i.e. where the real action takes place, back in the client's own work and life. However, the agenda may change radically from session to session as the client encounters new and current issues. The coach rarely knows what to expect at any given session, and needs to combine flexibility in dealing with twists and turns in the client's agenda while at the same time keeping aware of any consistent themes or patterns that underpin the issues raised.

Indeed it seems that the agenda the client brings initially is rarely the actual or ultimate agenda they need to work on. Coaching seems to be effective at least partly because its powerful questioning approach encourages a client to dig beneath the surface of an issue and uncover its true source and significance – coaching gets to the heart of an issue quickly.

Core coaching skills

Coaching can sound, superficially, like a conventional conversation. However, in reality it is highly structured, while retaining genuine humanity and a degree of spontaneity. Behind the apparent ease of conversation there are many distinct skills at play. To list them all would be too lengthy for the purposes of this book but there are some that are indispensable. These include rapport-building (the subject of an entire chapter in this book), attentive listening, agenda-building, offering feedback, asking powerful (as opposed to conventional) questions, summarizing, challenging and interrupting. There are numerous books that offer excellent introductions and instructions on these core skills.

What is NLP?

I first encountered NLP in 1988. I had just somewhat recklessly packed in a ten-year career as a social worker, and landed a new and exciting job as a management trainer working at Brathay Hall, the development centre in the Lake District. The social work experience, after a promising start, had eventually drained, disappointed and dispirited me. Within a few days of beginning at Brathay I began, along with all the other training staff, an in-house NLP Practitioner course. I had no idea what this was really about. I had had very little personal development training hitherto and did not even know the extent of my own ignorance in the area; to use the training jargon – I didn't know what I didn't know. I felt threatened and vulnerable and in the first couple of days of the NLP training I probably behaved fairly badly – cynical, defensive and dismissive. On about the third day the trainer took me to one side to discuss my apparent resistance. The upshot of this was me saying something along the lines of: 'OK, prove it works.'

The trainer asked me what evidence I would need to be convinced that NLP 'works'. The big issue I had at the time was fear of heights: there I was working in an outdoor-based management training centre, where almost every day I was being trained in the necessary skills to work with groups in the outdoors, frequently in the mountains, and on rock climbing and abseiling sites, and I was terrified of heights! My fear was intensified by what was at stake: having thrown in my career in social work it felt to me that every episode of heights-based activity and training carried with it not only intrinsic physical risks but also the risk of career failure – a personal script that led very quickly in my imagination to visions of the gutter.

I challenged the NLP trainer to do something about this. He took me through a complex process of vivid imagery to do with my fundamental fears in life overall and their relation to heights. At the end of this process he asked me to imagine myself in a particularly frightening heights situation – a visualization that previously had produced in me a genuinely phobic response. I did the visualization and noticed something missing: the terror had gone, replaced by a rather numb, much lower-level fear. The very next day, I climbed up onto Striding Edge, a steep arête, and the scene of my first real heights terror, aged about 12. To be honest I still found it rather frightening, but I was at least able to cope with it and not be frozen to the spot with terror as I would doubtless have been otherwise. I walked the ridge in both directions, something that had been unimaginably frightening hitherto.

The consequence of this one NLP session was that I was able to stay working at Brathay. Doubtless my colleagues there from that time will remember me as one of the least daring outdoorsmen to have ever worked in the industry, but at least I was able to get by, to complete the safety training required and to take my place on expeditions and other vertigo-inducing activities without collapsing with terror every day. Therefore, my career in training was saved, and I was convinced about NLP. From that day on I absorbed the NLP training like a sponge and subsequently helped as an assistant on a couple more practitioner courses to make sure I had really got it.

The benefits of the learning were to galvanize my life and career, giving both their biggest boost to date. I became positive, goal-focused and far more resourceful as a trainer and in business. I have a lot to thank the trainer for at that time in my life.

Later experiences in NLP, while continuing on a broadly generative path, have unfortunately held some disappointments as well as delights, not so much to do with the techniques themselves as with the style of training and indeed some of the individual trainers involved. I had a deeply disappointing experience on my master practitioner course, where one of the trainers was a nasty bully. My most recent exposure to NLP training earlier this year I found shocking: the trainer struck me as manipulative, egotistical and obsessed with money. However, he did keep hammering home the message that all perception of external reality was a projection of internal issues so maybe it (he) was my fault.

The picture I have of the NLP 'industry' is one of something dynamic and positive but also tainted in places by perceptions of factionalism, ego-driven conflict, legal disputes and commercial greed. What is more, the rather grandiose-sounding claims made on behalf of NLP by some practitioners as something that can cure all phobias at a stroke and perform other 'miracles' do not seem to me to be reflected in daily experience or a significantly happier population. I know some of these cures work for some people some of the time but I rarely come across people who tell tales of NLP transforming their lives in the way it did mine. Even as a fan and practitioner myself I would certainly caution anyone against swallowing NLP uncritically. The key is to be able to identify those who work well and ethically with NLP – thankfully, they can be found.

It is interesting to reflect upon NLP as a social phenomenon. I have heard several people liken it to a modern secular religion, and the analogy does stand up in some ways. There are founding father figures of the Moses type in Bandler, Grinder and others. There is a version of the Ten Commandments (the NLP presuppositions). There is certainly something resembling a priest-hood, and some of the more flamboyant trainers have begun to resemble prophets and gurus with cadres of 'disciples' in tow. There is something of alchemy in the blend too – a mixture of the promise of transformation with the increasing esotericism of techniques the higher you go up the hierarchy. I am, frankly, personally suspicious of some of this. I dislike anything that smacks of manipulation, and there is no doubt that on some of the large-scale training events you experience manipulative techniques such as powerfully suggestive music used specifically to trigger certain planned types of response. I also have concerns about the patent personal inauthenticity of some of these 'guru' trainers – there are times when they seem deeply incongruent in their behaviour. I have heard numerous attendees of practitioner courses who have experienced the personality and approach of the trainers as a block to their learning – they have had to overcome their personal distaste for the trainer in order to learn the skills on offer. There is no doubt, however, that these large-scale events represent a successful business model – some courses have hundreds of participants, each paying thousands of pounds. Sometimes it is hard not to think of parts of the NLP industry as get-rich-quick schemes.

But I remain a fan and a practitioner. On the more positive side I know personally many excellent practitioners who incorporate their NLP training into their own coaching, teaching, counselling or training practices with great effect, and who operate both ethically and humbly. I think a sound guideline if you are looking for an NLP trainer is to check their level of humility and authenticity, and their sense of being grounded in reality. They need to be able to 'walk the talk', i.e. relate to people authentically: if you have any doubts about the character and personality of any prospective trainer I would certainly pay attention to those doubts, no matter how dazzling the oratory or how exquisite the technique they offer. Most training NLP companies offer 'taster' events and I would certainly advocate experiencing these before signing up to a practitioner course which usually lasts around twenty days.

NLP in some ways becomes a way of life in that it is so engaged with the deeper self in terms of attitudes, assumptions, values and beliefs. When writing about specific tools and techniques within NLP it is important to remember that none of these techniques exists in isolation from the rest of NLP – the *presuppositions* unite them all in a theoretical way, but the practitioner can only use NLP effectively if the techniques are fully integrated into themselves in a congruent fashion. In practice therefore it is not appropriate to think of using NLP 'techniques' as a doctor might prescribe a medicine. The *relationship* between coach and client is at the heart of coaching with or without NLP: NLP is about helping the minds of both client and coach to work at their most effective, a set of processes and assumptions designed to help them both be at their most resourceful and for the relationship itself to enhance the resourcefulness of them both. When coaching is going at its best the coach and the client work as a unit and the learning is a two-way process. I would find it impossible to be an effective coach if I were not learning from my clients all the time.

Origins of NLP

NLP, or Neuro-Linguistic Programming, originated in California in the 1970s. This fact alone creates suspicion in the eyes of many British managers, who often have a strongly developed scepticism about anything 'psychological', and even more particularly about anything *Californian* and psychological. The originators were Richard Bandler, a mathematician, and John Grinder, a linguistics professor. Originally, they looked at the communications skills used by a selection of outstandingly successful therapists, with a view to establishing specifically *how* they were able to achieve success in helping clients to make positive changes in their lives. They and a group of colleagues and students tried to establish an explicit model of just how excellent communicators were able to achieve their results. Nevertheless even the experts and founders of NLP offer different definitions:

> NLP is an accelerated learning strategy for the detection and utilization of patterns in the world. (John Grinder)

> NLP is whatever works. (Robert Dilts)

> NLP is an attitude and a methodology, which leaves behind a trail of techniques. (Richard Bandler)

> NLP is the systematic study of human communication. (Alex von Uhde)

The actual term 'Neuro-Linguistic Programming' arises from three main areas of study:

1. Neurology: the mind and how we think.
2. Linguistics: how we use language and how it affects us.
3. Programming: how we sequence our actions.

The essence of their approach was pragmatic and results-oriented rather than theoretical. Richard Bandler succinctly described NLP as a process of helping people to learn how to use their brains more effectively – to run their brains rather than letting their brains run them. They initially sought to discover what actually worked in achieving positive results for therapy clients, by examining the links between the actual behaviours of the therapist and the thoughts and feelings of the clients themselves. The essence of this learning was that excellence in the communication field had *clear structures*. They sought to discover these structures and then to teach them. The underpinning attitudes they brought of curiosity and pragmatism have resulted in ideas, models and techniques based on the observed realities of how people think and behave.

This core idea, usually referred to as *modelling*, is based on a principle that, once something can be described with sufficient clarity and precision, it can be taught and learned. I do not think NLP can be effectively labelled as a static entity or a body of knowledge. I think of it as a process of enquiry into what works for individuals, resulting in new and teachable/learnable models and strategies.

NLP is about choice

NLP holds that 'reality' is not an objective construct, something 'out there', but something that people construct individually from their own perceptions and thinking (not a unique proposition in philosophical terms, but one that NLP seeks to place in the realms of practical action). It follows that there are no two identical versions of reality and that we all experience what we *call* reality somewhat differently. Events are not only perceived differently by each of us but they also carry different *meanings* at the level of values and beliefs. A core contention of NLP is that if 'reality' is individually constructed then individuals can have *choice* in how they interpret and respond to things outside themselves and how they manage their internal experience. Choice is at the heart of NLP.

> How many people are trapped in their everyday habits: part numb, part frightened, part indifferent? To have a better life we must keep choosing how we are living. (Albert Einstein)

Of course, choice and change can be scary. This is particularly so if people think that by *choosing* they are *losing*. A good principle of helping people to work to make changes is to offer reassurance that nothing is being taken away – only choices added.

NLP studies how we construct our internal experiences and make our personal version of 'reality'. This includes how we think about, and even create, our values and beliefs, how we create our emotional states and create meaning in our lives. A clear focus for this in NLP is our use of the five sensory systems: seeing, hearing, feeling, smelling and tasting. Each of us uses these with different degrees of emphasis and with our own unique internal grammar and syntax of sensory experience. NLP teaches that we can grow increasingly aware of our patterns of perception and interpretation, and in so doing can create the possibility of choosing patterns that are more effective for ourselves, and help others to do so too. This is one of the most radical propositions that NLP offers, and one that separates it out as a practical developmental tool.

How NLP and coaching work together

There is no doubt that NLP is having a profound influence upon the development of coaching practice. NLP techniques are taught wholesale on some coaching courses, without necessarily being labelled as such. In some cases it can be hard to see the join and there are numerous coaches for whom NLP is already part of a core methodology.

The overlaps in terms of practical techniques are rooted in some fundamental similarities at the level of core principles of practice. NLP is underpinned by a set of operating assumptions or principles called 'presuppositions' in NLP circles. There is a fascinating degree of overlap and compatibility between the presuppositions used by NLP practitioners and the principles we use in coaching. As with our coaching principles, NLP presuppositions are intended to operate not as intellectual truths but as essential attitudes and assumptions. So crucial are these presuppositions to NLP that they form a foundation of attitude and assumption without which NLP would have no binding structure. I include a chapter on this specific subject.

Just as the presuppositions and principles of coaching are compatible, so are the practical methodologies. From my point of view of seeking to practise integrated, NLP-accented coaching, it is getting harder and harder to see the join. So: NLP and coaching together – a powerful combination producing practical, robust results in an enjoyable and empowering way.

Contracting with clients using NLP

Some skills and techniques in coaching can be approached in numerous ways, and it is always useful to have a wide repertoire of approaches whatever their provenance. It is essential in coaching to have a clear, mutually agreed contract in place between client and coach – something that sets in place explicitly exactly how they are going to work, and what their mutual expectations are. Coaching can founder for lack of clarity at the outset, and this is a step in the coaching process that simply cannot be skimped. At the very least, coach and client should engage with the following questions:

- What must you get from the coaching?
- How will you know when you've got it?
- How can I as coach help you to get what you need?
- How can you help yourself to get what you need?

- How might you/we/I sabotage the process?
- How will you/we/I ensure this does not happen?

A useful addition to contracting technique, taken explicitly from NLP, is called *future pacing*. This technique draws on the work of seminal medical hypnotherapist Milton Eriksson. One of the many stories told about Eriksson involved his conversation with a mentally ill patient who had so far failed to respond to all treatments offered him. Eriksson opened his discussion with the patient by asking him to describe *when* he gets better! By so doing he created an explicit assumption that the patient *would* get better. The patient responded by describing a time some years in the future when he felt he would have recovered. Eriksson then asked him to imagine he was actually at that future point in time, looking back on the intervening years, and asked him what the treatment had been that cured him. The patient described the steps needed, and the treatment programme was able to begin . . .

Future pacing

A simple adaptation of the technique called 'future pacing' works extremely well in coaching. At your first session, ask your client to imagine they are leaving their final session with you. (You may wish to set the expectation in advance that you are going to ask them to do something a little unorthodox.) Get them to imagine that, as they are leaving the last session, they are reflecting on how valuable the sessions have been – in fact far exceeding their wildest expectations. (Check with them that they are actually allowing themselves to do this – perhaps pointing out how valuable mental rehearsal is in creating positive performance.) Finally, ask them the key questions: 'So, just what did *we* do to create this success? How did *we* work together, specifically, to be so successful?' Make sure the client always answers in the past tense, using phrases such as: 'We tackled the really tough issues' or 'You challenged me hard'. It is useful at the end of this process just to summarize what it is the client intuitively knows will work for them. The key to the technique is that it taps into the intuitive wisdom of the client, providing a simple but elegant structure that allows this wisdom free expression. It also offers the client a means to do some positive mental rehearsal, in itself a powerful tool.

I have yet to meet a client who will not respond to this exercise with useful insight into what is going to make the sessions work *for them*. Note that the questioning itself implies a partnership approach.

Future pacing can also be useful at other points in the coaching process, for example in finding ways forward when the client might feel temporarily stuck.

It would be wrong, however, to think of coaching as merely the *application* of skills or a *management* of principles and processes. At the heart of coaching is a human relationship, sometimes one as close as business or even social protocol allows to a touching of souls. The coach is in a hugely privileged position, working in partnership with someone who has chosen to act positively on the belief that something fundamentally important in their life and/or work can be improved by working with you as a coach. Often the client in this relationship is at their most vulnerable and open at the very point when you as a coach are working with them to be at their most resourceful. Thus, polar extremes of vulnerability and empowerment can be present in the same room, at the same time and in the same person, all in the coach's privileged presence.

All of this is in dynamic flux and needs absolute care of judgement on the coach's part in balancing the many apparent (and sometimes hidden) contradictory drivers, for example:

- the need to balance learning and the building of understanding with the drive for change and action
- the need to support the client in their vulnerability and yet challenge them hard to achieve their goals
- the need to convey respect and empathy while not colluding with the client
- the need to tackle issues holistically while focusing on actions that may be relevant only in a specific context.

The coach should never, ever be a set of techniques in search of an issue to practise on. If in doubt as to what to do, ask the client what they think they need, remembering they are not there to be 'fixed' by you but to work alongside you. Trust that by listening attentively, asking powerful questions and sticking to the principles of coaching and the presuppositions of NLP, you will be helping the client to become more resourceful.

In the following chapters I describe a number of scenarios drawn from years of coaching in which NLP techniques have helped to produce great results for the client. Please note that the clients' names are in all cases fictional, and sometimes the examples are composites: but in every case the issue was a real one brought by a real client or more than one client.

2 A solid foundation
The presuppositions of NLP

The presuppositions of NLP have developed over time as core attitudes and principles underpinning all approaches and techniques that NLP has spawned. They are *not intended as propositions of intellectual truth*, but as attitudes and assumptions consistent with resourceful thinking and behaviour. Their apparent simplicity, and their radical quality, sometimes provoke accusations of vague idealism, but in reality they are extremely pragmatic, and from the coach's perspective absolutely invaluable in finding keys to help clients unlock needed resources. Each of the presuppositions is independently useful, but they are at their most powerful when linked together to create a framework and structure of mutually reinforcing attitudes and assumptions.

Numerous practitioners have developed and created these presuppositions over the years, and new ones emerge for discussion frequently. You only have to tap in 'NLP presuppositions' on Google (28,200 sites connected to the subject at the last look) to be met with a demonstration of the interest that NLP presuppositions create. The formulations vary somewhat depending upon which author you read, but the fundamental presuppositions can be described as follows.

'The map is not the territory'

This presupposition sets out the idea that the way we experience the world is not the way the world actually is, but is our interpretation of it. In simple terms, this means we are always to some degree separated from 'reality'. We tend to create, and respond to, our personal 'map' rather than relating directly to the world as it occurs in the present. Our 'maps' are at one level composed of our direct sensory experience, but they are also attempts to put meaning, understanding and structure around this experience. This is a useful thing to a point, of course – we need a degree of meaning and structure in order to operate in the world at all. However, the downside of our map-making is that no matter how detailed the map is, it is never wholly accurate or complete – the map is not actually the place it depicts. In time, we tend to come to believe that the map *is* the territory – that the world is actually how we represent it to ourselves. This is very significant in terms of how we see things, in particular the words and actions of other people (each of whom is, of course, the creator of their own map), and how we judge and respond to them.

We have, according to this presupposition, *choice* as to how we respond and behave in relation to our 'maps'. To begin with, we can be aware that the map is just that – a representation, not reality itself. If our map is making us unhappy in some way, for example in how we are judging and responding to the behaviour of others who do not behave in a way consistent with our map, we can choose to learn new responses. In coaching, many clients are unhappy with the behaviours of other people in their work and lives: they often have clear views about how these others 'ought' to behave. The coach has the possibility of working through these issues on the basis of the presupposition. To begin with, the coach can draw the client's attention to the very fact that how they are interpreting something is not an objective reality, but a construction. This in itself can be helpful for some clients. Over and above this, coaches can work with clients to look at how accurate and reliable their maps are – for example, at the formative experiences and influences that helped create the maps in the first place – and help them put in place more useful assumptions.

The coach can also help the client to understand that the map is distancing them from what is actually going on or happening around them rather than focusing on how things 'ought' to be: they can help clients to be more 'present', that is, more responsive to what is actually going on rather than responding to their 'pre-judged' outlook.

Another positive for the coach arising out of this presupposition is that it is usually easier to help someone change their personal 'map' of reality than to collude in their attempts to change the world. Many people are made unhappy because the world is not to their liking, but the only place a real change can be made is inside the head – to how a person both sees and responds to the world. There was a *Big Issue* seller who operated in central London some years ago. He was particularly well organized, and plied his trade next to a small stall made of something like milk crates, against which he would position a placard outlining his 'Thought for the Day'. One day his placard read: 'Happiness is not about what happens to you: it is about what you *do* about what happens to you.' This encapsulates one of the key aspects of the presupposition: that we *always* have choice about how we interpret and respond to our circumstances. This is so important in working with 'stuck' clients, who can see no way forward on their issue: if the coach is able to help the client see that the way they are seeing the issue *is* the issue, or at least part of it, then the client can find ways of redrawing their 'map' to make the issue less of an obstacle than they thought it was.

Another dimension of this powerful presupposition is that of *rapport*. As discussed in its own chapter, rapport skills are at the heart of successful relationships. The person who is aware that everyone is experiencing and understanding the world in often radically different ways has an enormous head-start when it comes to the creation of rapport with a wide range of people. Beyond this, the ability to 'tune in' (or, to use the NLP jargon, 'calibrate') to someone else and thus find clues in their language and behaviour as to how they are experiencing themselves and understanding the world allows one to adjust one's own language and behaviour in ways that are likely to create rapport: but all this starts from the fundamental assumption that our, and their, maps are *not* the territory.

For the NLP coach the process of constantly checking in on the 'maps' of our clients is an essential part of our approach. The maps include the sensory patterns used by the clients, their word usage and its indicators of values, beliefs and assumptions, body language and indeed the whole way the client is communicating – including what they are not saying.

'If one person can do something, other people can learn to do it'

We can learn an achiever's mental 'map' and make it our own. This is about the important part of NLP known as *modelling*. Modelling is about identifying what it is that people who are successful in some behaviour or field actually and *specifically* do that helps them to be successful. When the critical differences have been recognized and identified they can be learned or taught – given sufficient motivation and commitment on the part of the learner.

For me the real meat of this presupposition is the challenge it creates for those clients who believe or assume they are unable to achieve to the degree of success they would wish for in a given area. Many clients assume that others are successful because they have special talents or gifts that set them apart. The reality is that every talent has a structure and a syntax, or sequence, of sensory events and behaviours. The challenge is often to be able to break these skills down into small enough chunks that they can be learned.

Chris

An example from recent coaching experience is that of Chris, a client from the hospitality industry who wanted to be a more effective public speaker but did not believe she had the required 'talent'. My approach with her was to ask her to identify a selection of speakers from the public arena she personally admired, and engage with her in analysing in some detail just how they got the results they got. The results were a minor revelation for Chris – she realized, after quite a lot of analytical work, that attributes she had labelled as 'presence' or 'charisma' were in fact composed of easily replicable behaviours such as pausing, standing still and sweeping the audience with her eyes. It was a revelation to her that what she had thought of as 'special' talents were in fact easily within her power to learn, and because she had the motivation and commitment, she went on to learn them.

This presupposition is not a blank cheque, however: no one is saying that absolutely everyone can learn to do absolutely everything. Often, a particular degree of, say, intelligence or physical capability is required. But even the apparently least able in a given area can make great strides towards improvements and success if they are willing to put in the effort of analysis and to try out new behaviours. This is where the coach can be of huge help in supporting and challenging clients to find resources within themselves they may not have been aware of – the essence of coaching.

'If you go on doing what you are currently doing you are likely to go on getting the same results as you are getting now'

There is a common proverb that goes: 'If at first you don't succeed, try, try, again.' We read as children how Robert the Bruce was inspired by a dogged spider to resume his own struggle. At the heart of this story is the principle of persistence. The problem with this otherwise admirable principle is that if we persist in actions or behaviours that are not working for us, they are likely to continue not to work for us no matter how often we try them. We sometimes need more than persistence alone to succeed, because circumstances change all the time, and what has worked for us in the past might have a law of diminishing returns. If you shout at the children to behave, and they don't, then shouting louder or more often is unlikely to have much effect.

This is why making a decision on the basis that 'that's the way we have always done it' is often the prelude to failure. The key here is to vary your behaviour until you get what you want, rather than do more of what is not working. I see numerous managers who are puzzled and exhausted because the harder they work, the less success they are getting in their jobs: at some point in their careers they learned that working hard increased their chances of success, but they did not realize that a behaviour that gets them to a certain point may actually prevent them from making progress to the next stage. Continuing in homily mode, in behavioural terms 'the very thing that makes you rich can make you poor'.

For the coach, the presupposition therefore translates into the practice of encouraging/challenging/supporting clients to try new behaviours and approaches where the old ones are no longer working as well as they did.

Glynn

A recent example in my own coaching was Glynn, a manager in a technical part of a broadcasting organization. For years I had worked with Glynn on various projects – team-building events, facilitating away-days and so on. He had always had something of an abrasive personal style: not abusive in any way, but quite argumentative and forceful in putting his views across. Unfortunately, he was not so strong on follow-through: once the argument was 'won' in principle he tended not to go on and enforce his decision with his staff. In effect, his bark was much worse than his bite. Over the years his staff had come to read his behaviour and to play up to it, resulting in two negatives for Glynn: his views and 'decisions' tended to be largely ignored, and as his frustration grew, so did his reputation as a poor communicator. However, he had come to believe that his forthright manner was his only real strength in managing a demanding set of staff. In our coaching we gradually worked round to the ideas of trying a totally different approach, in effect the reverse of what had long since ceased to be effective. Glynn agreed to try a new approach that involved a radical change to his communication style, with far more emphasis on listening, combined with relentless though calm insistence on his decisions being implemented. To begin with we focused on small, almost trivial decisions, but gradually worked up to the much more important ones. Glynn's staff came to learn that his decisions were not to be ignored, and gradually came to appreciate his much more receptive communication style.

'Your mind and your body are indivisible parts of the same interactive system'

For some time in the West the medical profession in particular took an approach to healing based on increasing knowledge of the functioning of the body's constituent parts. This led to a symptom-led approach in which the specific part of the body showing the distress was treated. This was mirrored by a general scientific preoccupation with discovering and isolating smaller and smaller particles of matter. Only in the last couple of decades has practical, verifiable scientific evidence emerged to show beyond doubt that mental activity and the functions of the body are integrally linked – at the same time as science is generally adopting whole-system thinking as the norm. So, for example, mental stress can now be linked to the weakening of the immune system and thus a lowering of general health, and the existence of 'psychosomatic' (literally 'of mind and body') illness is widely accepted.

From the coach's point of view this presupposition, when translated into practical applications, adds an extremely important dimension to the ways in which clients can be supported in becoming more resourceful. At its simplest, it is important for the coach to pay attention to the physical aspects of their client's behaviour. Does the body language match up with the words being spoken, for example? How resourceful can a client really feel if their body is slumped and their eyes are constantly on the ground? Clients who seem rooted to a problem-focus in their thinking and speaking will almost certainly reflect this in some aspect of their physical presentation. It is open to the coach to offer feedback on this as a means of encouraging a more positive physical state. It is also part of the coach's skill to model a more helpful physical presentation by matching pacing and leading the client's physical being. (More on this in Chapter 3.)

More radical interventions are available too. You might try the following exercise for yourself. Think of an issue of your own that you consider pro- blematical. As you think about the issue, adopt a slumped, negative posture with eyes looking at the ground. Pay attention to what the problem looks like, sounds like and feels like to you. Next, just go for a walk outside: coach yourself on walking to the absolute peak of enjoyment, making any adjust- ments you see fit to breathing, pace, rhythm, etc. While you are continuing to walk in this optimum way, mentally revisit the problem you first thought of *while maintaining the perfect walking*. Notice the difference in the way the 'problem' looks, feels and sounds. I guarantee there will be changes.

You may choose at some point to offer this experience to one or more of your clients (after all, who said coaching has to be two people sitting in a room all the time?).

'People have all the resources they need'

By *resources* we generally refer to skills, states, qualities and attributes. Examples that come up frequently in coaching include confidence, courage and compassion (three very important 'co' examples within coaching). The presupposition does *not* literally mean that anybody can achieve anything whatsoever, but rather points to the fact that the basic building blocks of our experiences in life – our perceptions, responses and actions – form the basis of our mental and even physical resources, and that these are far more complete than we sometimes think when we perceive ourselves to be in 'resource deficit'.

From a coach's point of view, to believe explicitly or implicitly the opposite presupposition, i.e. that we are all fundamentally limited in our resourcefulness, has two important negative consequences or likely coaching outcomes: (1) we will stop looking for resources in our clients, and (2) our negative expectations will transmit themselves to our clients at conscious and unconscious levels.

Of course, in order to be able to use a resource you must first be aware that you have it. NLP is rich in 'resource-locating' techniques (many of which, such as the meta-mirror, anchoring and time-line therapy are described in this book). Each of them in some way reconnects the client with some personal resource that he or she has definitely had access to in their lives but which appears to them now to be temporarily unavailable.

You also need to know how to use the resources you possess appropriately and in the right context: a coruscating wit is perhaps not appropriate in situations calling for tact and sensitivity, for example.

'You cannot *not* communicate'

We are always communicating, at least non-verbally, and words are often the least important part. We are even influencing others when we are not physically there. If you doubt this, consider how you think or feel about a scary or difficult boss or colleague, and how these thoughts and feelings subtly influence your behaviour towards them in advance of any contact with them: or think about the positive feelings and responses you have for an absent friend. Even some of our thought processes (specifically, whether we are processing visually, auditorily or kinaesthetically, for example) are revealed to others in our eyes, voice, postures and body movements. By the same token we influence others and have impact on them even if we choose to withdraw 'direct' communication in words – I have seen many a meeting dominated by someone who stays silent throughout.

One implication of this is for our responsibilities as communicators. I once worked as coach with a manager whose personal style was tight-lipped, even secretive. He felt his behaviour to be appropriate and even heroic – he saw himself as shouldering all the burdens of his department and protecting his staff from having to worry about pressures he was dealing with alone. He was shocked to get feedback from his staff that described him as scary, aloof and untrusting. The fact that they never knew exactly what he was thinking about led them to speculate and fantasize – and this is almost always a negative experience. As psychologist Carl Rogers says, a lack of feedback is inherently punishing at a psychological level – not knowing is not a neutral state.

'The meaning of your communication is the response that you get'

This means that whatever you *think* is the meaning of the message you are sending out to others when you communicate, or whatever its *intent*, the real meaning of the message is what people actually receive – the meaning *they* attach to it. People will respond to what they *think* you mean, which may or may not be an accurate interpretation of your intended meaning. And of course, much of your communication is contained in its non-verbal aspects, particularly communication about, or involving, any degree of feeling or emotion. Therefore, if we aspire to communicate effectively as coaches we must be constantly aware of other people's responses to what we are saying (both their verbal and non-verbal responses) and adjust our communication accordingly, rather than assume they will automatically understand what we mean them to understand.

This is a challenging proposition for coaches and clients alike. I have encountered many managers who in coaching sessions express their frustration at being 'misunderstood' by their staff or colleagues. One such manager described how upset he was at getting feedback that he was constantly critical of his staff. When we looked at his actual behaviour, he admitted that a high proportion of his words were indeed critical, but he in fact felt extremely positive about most of their work. 'Surely they realize I love 99 per cent of what they do?' he said once. Unfortunately for him, they did not, and it took a nasty shock in the form of some very blunt feedback to alert him to the reality of how his communication was being received. This presupposition acts as a powerful stimulus for the coach in helping clients to recognize that the responsibility for being understood rests primarily with them.

'Change makes change'

When you make a change in coaching it is important to realize that the change, however positive, has consequences for the rest of your personal system – both inside yourself and outside yourself. So coaches need to think about change for their clients holistically, and help clients to think through the whole-system implications of even the most apparently beneficial change. As a simple example, if in coaching a client decides to go for a promotion, one of the ways in which the coach can help is to get the client to think through all the other things that might change, or need to change, if they are successful – work patterns, relationships with colleagues and so forth: even things in the personal or domestic realm may experience relatively subtle changes that need to be thought through or acted upon.

Another dimension of this presupposition is the concept that in order to change behaviour in others we must makes changes ourselves – something that becomes very clear in exercises such as the meta-mirror. Many clients come to coaching with the initial assumption that their coaching need is to change someone else in some way. In coaching, change is focused on what *you* need to change: if you find yourself being bullied at work, for example, the core to changing the situation is to do with how you yourself behave rather than trying to change in any direct way how the bully acts.

'Every behaviour has a positive intention'

This is a presupposition that needs especially careful explanation for some people. The essential meaning is that every behaviour emanates at root from some positive need or desire on the part of the creator of the behaviour – whether or not it has positive *effects* for themselves or for others. The key idea is that everyone is fundamentally trying to serve, at the least, their *own* best interests through their behaviours: where the behaviour actually produces a negative result for themselves or others it is because their choice of behaviour is wrong, not their intention. From those seeking to test this presupposition I have often been asked questions like 'What about Hitler? What was his positive intention in murdering millions?' I do not know anything about Hitler's psyche and could not presume to know exactly what he was trying to do for himself or for his country: if forced to speculate, I would ask what he *might* have been trying to get out of it – perhaps, as with so many bullies, a sense of reassurance or of significance. However, if I were with an actual client whose behaviour was causing suffering for others I would ask myself, and them, just what their behaviour was *trying* to achieve in order to gain understanding before looking at more positive alternative choices. This is not about liberal relativism or any other form of ideological conviction on my part: it is about looking for practical options for more desirable ways of helping someone to satisfy their own needs in ways that may also benefit others.

The child who feels insecure or who needs more attention may resort to bullying or disruptive behaviour in the attempt to secure what they need, and we may, from an orthodox viewpoint, infer that their intention is 'bad' or 'evil' when in fact it is only the behaviour that needs to change – there is no need to demonize the child, nor is there any benefit to be gained from doing so. For the coach this means helping the client to recognize that their own behaviour is rooted in positive intention: if they can work out the intention of their behaviour, then they can look for more effective ways of getting the intention met. This does *not* mean that we need to approve or tolerate negative or antisocial behaviour in ourselves or others – it means only that we need to understand the basic positive intention of that behaviour in order look for better alternatives or choices.

Fortunately, in executive coaching the examples of this presupposition in action are rarely to do with such extreme behaviours as those referred to above. I recently worked with a very talented musician, Tom, whose confidence was so low he was unable to perform any more in public. He told me how his nervous behaviour had begun in infancy when, rather than risk the sharp disapproval of his father, who would shout criticism at him if he said, or did, anything the father perceived as 'wrong', he would retreat into silence and voluntary isolation. In later life the critical father 'became' the audience in his mind, and he grew extremely apprehensive about the disapproval he imagined his audience would express if he made a mistake during performance. He decided not to take the risk any more: with a huge sense of frustration he gave up public performance. One of the breakthroughs we were able to achieve in coaching was for him to realize that his nervous behaviour was not some kind of despicable disabling weakness in him (which was how he had thought about it for forty years) but was actually trying to do something positive for him: that is, it was trying to *protect* him. From this realization we were able to go on and look at how he might protect himself from actual or imagined criticism in other ways, and from there to look at other confidence-enhancing techniques. I was delighted to be invited to his comeback performance, at which he played brilliantly and without nervousness. By a stroke of irony or synchronicity, his father expressed approval for his playing (the first such approval he had ever uttered) just at the point that Tom had rid himself of the need for it.

'Every behaviour is appropriate in some context: and no behaviour is appropriate in every context'

This is another presupposition that can cause a degree of outrage until it is explained fully: 'Surely there are some things you should *never* do or say; surely there are some things you should *always* do?' say the outraged. 'Surely you should *never* be impolite, act aggressively, be selfish? Surely you should *always* think of others?'

What this presupposition is really saying is that we should allow ourselves to be more flexible in our behaviour, taking the cue for appropriateness from the *context* for the behaviour rather than from mere habit: just because something worked for us once upon a time, for example, does not mean it will work for us for ever or in every circumstance. There may be a context in which it is appropriate to be angry – for example, if someone has been bullying us. There may be contexts when being apparently selfish might be absolutely right – for example, in insisting on not being disturbed if you are trying to complete an important task. Similarly there are some behaviours someone might think are 'always' appropriate which are not: what is the point in being polite and patient if we are receiving very poor or rude customer service, for example?

The heart of the presupposition is the impetus it gives us to examine – and help our clients to examine – the behaviours and attitudes they just take for granted, with a view to increasing options and flexibility.

'There is no such thing as failure, only feedback'

When things do not work out quite as we intend we often interpret the result we get as failure. Sometimes the effect of the perception of results as failure is disheartening, or disappointing, leading us to never take the risk again or even to feel permanently bad about ourselves. This presupposition reminds us that 'failure' as a concept does not serve much purpose in most realms of behaviour, and that it is far more useful to see a situation that does not work out as a demonstration of exactly how *not* to do something in the future: Edison famously spoke of discovering a thousand sure-fire ways of *not* making a light bulb work before finding the right way.

By encouraging clients to view their experiences in this way, 'failure' can be routinely seen as opportunity to learn and to plan a different way of approaching something.

The presuppositions alongside the principles of coaching

It is useful to compare these presuppositions with the six principles of coaching described by Jenny Rogers (2004) in her book *Coaching Skills: A Handbook*. These are as follows:

1. The client is a resourceful person.
2. The coach's role is to spring loose the resourcefulness of the client.
3. The coach and the client work as equals.
4. The client sets the agenda.
5. The client is a whole person, work and home, past and present.
6. Coaching is about change.

These principles are very simple in essence but do in fact capture absolutely the core of how a coach should approach the task – *always* assuming the client has the answer or resource within themselves, *always* assuming that *they*, not the coach, decide what they need/want to work on, and that as 'whole people' the changes they want to make need to be worked through holistically. The NLP presuppositions are wholly consistent with these principles and add a degree of depth and radicalism that can help clients to think in whole new ways about themselves, their issues and about their potential for positive change.

3 Creating rapport in coaching

Coaching is a relationship that depends on a sense of committed and trusting partnership. Leaving aside the importance of treating clients with respect and courtesy, it is important to remember that clients frequently make themselves vulnerable by bringing to the coaching room issues where they do not currently feel at their most confident, empowered or resourceful: the coach needs to respond to this potential vulnerability with care, respect and sensitivity. The coach also faces the challenge of needing to create positive partnerships with a wide range of personalities and behaviours, adapting their own approach to suit the individual's personal style as far as possible. The first steps in any coaching partnership should be the creation of rapport between coach and client. Clients look for this factor, along with personal credibility, more than any other attribute, quality or skill in their coaches, and with good reason.

The issue of rapport in coaching is relevant at many levels: the issues that clients bring to the coaching room are often to do with relationships and personal effectiveness, and coaching using NLP can allow a client to learn an enormous amount about how to create rapport and build more positive relationships.

A lot of the early effort and research into NLP was on the subject of rapport: and NLP has built much of its reputation on its work in this area. Early research into the effectiveness of varying styles of psychotherapy brought about the realization that the critical success factor, regardless of the style of psychotherapy used, *was* the level of rapport between therapist and client. This led to much investigation into the nature of rapport and then to looking at how rapport skills could be modelled and taught.

This chapter looks at the following:

- The nature of rapport – what is it and how do you know you have got it?
- How do you as a coach go about creating rapport with your clients?
- How do you help your client to create rapport in their relationships?

What is rapport?

A common-sense view of rapport is that it is simply about *liking* someone or someone else *liking* you. However, there is more to it than this: as a coach it is not necessary actively to *like* your clients in the conventional sense, nor they you, but it is necessary to have a positive working relationship. Some people seem to rub along for many years without seemingly to actively like each other in the sense of sharing a fondness. There was a pub I used to go to in London where, for over ten years to my knowledge, but for many more according to folklore, two old men used to sit in the same seats every night and argue vehemently about everything and anything. To the casual observer their relationship was hostile, but the fact was they were virtually inseparable. In sporting contests opponents can hammer away at each other for hours and even days and yet at the end of a contest hug each other and drink beer together as mates. Some marital relationships seem to be based primarily on active disagreement but survive 'happily' for decades.

One view of rapport taken from NLP is that it is based on the principle of three 'Rs':

- respect
- recognition
- reassurance.

Respect

It is essential to create a climate of respect in the coaching room. Some clients feel a sense of embarrassment or even failure as they talk about their issues, and need the coach to convey respect for them in order that they can feel safe and supported. Frequently clients ask if their issues are 'typical' issues, the underlying fear being that there may be something amiss about them as clients for them to be bringing the issues they have. Respect is an essential part of the coaching climate, and without it, it is impossible to coach. Where the coach genuinely cannot respect the client, for example if the client persistently voices strong racist views, they should end the relationship. Having said this, the coach can still convey respect for the vast majority of the views and opinions of the client, even if they as coach do not happen to agree with them: at the deeper levels of values there will almost always be some alignment in any case. The coach can always convey respect for their client as a fellow human being.

Recognition

Recognition can be shown in a number of ways. The simplest and most fundamental way is for the coach to 'tune in' (or *calibrate*, to use the NLP jargon) at the physical level, altering your body language to be more like that of the clients. Other coaching skills that can help to convey this sense of recognition for the client include *summarizing* and *acknowledging*.

The *summary*, a staple tool in many forms of one-to-one work, is a very simple but effective way of showing you are present and attentive and that you have heard both the content and the *meaning* of what your client is telling you. You can summarize the content of what a client is saying and also the feeling they are expressing. This can also present the opportunity to reflect back the language the client is using, particularly their specific use of sensory-based words and any key metaphors used.

Acknowledgement is the act of pointing out to the client a significant resource you have noticed either in their behaviour in the present, or in an account of their actions outside the coaching room. It can be as simple as saying something like, 'You were very brave when you confronted your boss' or 'I would just like to say you are showing real tenacity in trying out this different way of approaching things'. When you *acknowledge* a strength or quality in the client, you are conveying respect for part of their 'being' or higher self.

Reassurance

By reassuring your client that it is OK to be themselves, and that it is OK for them to have their issue and not *currently* know how to make progress on it, you will be laying the foundations for progress. You can further reassure your clients by following the foundation principles of coaching, and the pre-suppositions of NLP, by letting them know you believe them to be resourceful people. It is important to work continuously on your own speech patterns in order to ensure that the presuppositions they contain are affirming for the client. There is a world of difference in saying something like 'So, let's continue to uncover the strengths you will be using to continue your progress' – a sentence suggesting an outcome focus and several positive presuppositions, as compared with something like 'Well, let's get started on trying to find the first steps to solving your problem' – a sentence that is problem-focused and full of negative presuppositions.

You can reassure powerfully by your own 'being' self, too: by listening attentively and by reacting calmly and confidently to what they tell you, you can show you are willing and able to help them make progress and that you believe them implicitly to have what it takes to do so.

Rapport is an activity

There is no noun that can convey the *active* nature of rapport. Rapport is similar to 'relationship' – people somehow think of their relationship as a 'thing' they 'possess' or 'have' rather than as a constant flux of ongoing behaviours. In actual fact there is no such 'thing' as a relationship, merely the sequence of active behaviours that go on between people. The degree to which a 'relationship' can be described as a static entity is probably a function of its habits – those behaviours that are repeated regularly enough for distinct patterns to be established – the habits of relating. The habits lead to the creation of overall perceptions, beliefs and judgements about the relating process – in short, what it means and how it is valued.

The smallest of behaviours in other people, even unconscious ones, can have deep impact on our beliefs and values, and as coaches we need to have the maximum possible awareness of our own behaviours, even the apparently trivial ones, and their potential effect on our clients. For example, I was once coached by someone who would look at the clock on the table in front of him every few minutes, and who sometimes moved his eyes *just a little bit* from side to side as I was speaking. I began to develop a feeling that he was impatient to end the sessions, and that he was uninterested in listening to what I had to say. I was distracted and even offended by this behaviour. When I raised it with him he was shocked: he assured me that his clock-watching was intended to make sure he could structure the session properly, and the eye movements were to do with him thinking about how his next question should be formulated. Both behaviours were, from his point of view, directed at my wellbeing, but the actual effect on me was negative. I also remember a client of mine who, out of the blue, said to me in an angry voice, 'Can you *please* stop using the word "actually" all the time?' It appeared that he interpreted my use of the word as patronizing, whereas I, far from intending to patronize, had not even been aware that I was using the word at all, actually.

Rapport is not necessarily 'natural'

Another 'common-sense' assumption is that rapport somehow occurs 'naturally' or not at all. It is true that most of us find it easier to create rapport with some people than others: but NLP holds that rapport, as a sequence of active behaviours, can be modelled and learned, and that it is theoretically possible to learn how to create rapport with virtually anybody.

When participants on our coaching courses put forward the view that rapport is, and should be, a 'natural' phenomenon, we sometimes ask them how they *know* they have rapport with someone. Most people respond to this with a statement about *feeling*. But when asked what *creates* the feeling, the response is almost invariably about what they *see* and *hear* from the other person and what goes on between them. Ultimately the degree of rapport is a consequence of sequences of observable behaviours and our response to them at the level of *meaning – values and beliefs*.

However, we do not always *consciously* observe the relevant behaviours – we tend to process them primarily at an unconscious level. It follows that if you can learn to observe and pay conscious attention to behaviours in others and in yourself, you can begin to learn the behaviours that lead to the creation of rapport. As for the 'naturalness' of our social behaviours, what feels *natural* is generally what is in fact just *habitual*. There was a time in our early lives when we were all taught the basic rules of courtesy (our p's and q's, for example), and these behaviours only began to feel natural after a lot of reminders and practice. We are not naturally gifted with knowledge of basic table manners – we have to learn them. The whole field of management development is filled with behavioural skills that for many managers need to be learned but which are taken for granted as being required: for example, giving feedback, making positive presentations or learning to answer questions effectively in public. Thus it is with rapport skills: we pick up some from observation and habit but because rapport is not something to which many of us pay conscious attention, we do not always know what else there is to learn. So, in order to learn and acquire a wider range of skills, we first need to understand what we don't yet know about the specific behaviours that create rapport.

Matching

Matching is what is meant by 'tuning in' (to use an aural metaphor) or *calibrating* to an aspect of someone else's body language, or use of voice, and adjusting your own to be more *like* the other person. This is what often happens in social situations: when we walk into a party it feels 'natural' to gravitate to the people we judge to be somehow compatible with us – and often this compatibility is assessed by unconscious recognition of similarity of body language. We have to make decisions quite quickly in all walks of life about whether we want or need to be with one sort of person rather than another: at times this ability to make quick 'instinctual' decisions about other people can be important for our very survival. It is in this literal sense that rapport is indeed about 'liking' someone else – we tend to 'like' those people who in some sense show they are 'like' us. Of course, other people are responding to us in just the same 'instinctive' way, and learning to 'match' can help to ensure you are accepted by far more people and in a much wider range of situations than you might hitherto have realized.

Many of our coaching students are able to take in this concept at an intellectual level easily, and indeed it is not unique to NLP. Sometimes they wonder what the 'big deal' is. What we often find, though, is that for them to become adept at a *practical* level they really need to work at it – to make their responses work in a way that looks and feels authentic. Authenticity is the key here – once the skills have been learned, practised and fully integrated, they feel as 'natural' as saying please and thank you. The trick is to develop speed and accuracy of response, and this only happens with a lot of conscious practice and a lot of feedback. There is no substitute for developing these skills if you want to develop rapport with your clients, or anyone else for that matter: this is an area where 'clunkiness' of technique is very likely to hamper the coaching relationship. (An example: I recently assessed a student on a coaching course who began his meeting with a brand-new client with the words, 'Right, let's start off with a bit of rapport then . . .' – the response was not exactly love at first sight.)

When I meet a client, my first coaching action is to pay real 'in-the-moment' attention to them. How do they look and sound? What is their energy level like? What (if I have worked with them before) is different about them from last time? This has to be a very quick process in order that I can adjust my own behaviour to theirs quickly enough to create a natural feeling of rapport at the basic physical level.

In deciding what to 'tune in' to and match, there is a wide range of choice. In body language terms alone there are the following:

- posture
- gesture
- facial expression
- level of muscle tension
- breathing – rate and depth
- eye contact – type of and amount of it
- speed of movement
- rhythm
- energy levels.

My own approach is to focus instantly on the basic energy and rhythm of the other person and respond quickly to that, closely followed by posture and facial expression. With this foundation in place it is possible to calibrate to the other dimensions of their physical presentation at more leisure.

Then there is voice. You may choose to pay *conscious* attention to one or more of the following (although you can be sure your unconscious mind will be paying attention to the rest):

- tone
- volume

- pitch
- accent
- speed
- rhythm.

Because so much of coaching is about talking, it is particularly important to pay close attention to how your speech matches up to that of your clients. This is even beyond any consideration of the *content* of what they are saying.

The above are really just shortlists – there are many minutiae.

Interpreting body language

I find it useful to direct our coaching students away from the idea that particular body language 'means' something specific. It is not *necessarily* the case, for example, that folded arms indicate defensiveness – a popular assumption. I fold my arms a lot, even while watching TV or sitting in the bath, because I find this posture helps me relax (I admit this is a weird habit). You may have seen the television advert in which the lone traveller, enjoying his meal in a South American shanty cantina, inadvertently offends the chef by making the 'O' sign with finger and thumb – a gesture generally associated in the West with warm approval, but a huge insult in that particular culture. Similarly, it is not necessarily the case that all people enjoy lots of unblinking, direct eye contact – another popular generalization. It is important to be aware of the cultural habits of societies other than our own: most research on body language – the research that produces the majority of the popular beliefs about meaning and body language – has been conducted in the Western cultures of Europe, the United States and Australia.

Of course, some people are practised and accomplished at this matching skill without the benefit of NLP or coaching skills training. I have a friend who spent three years travelling the remotest corners of the world by bicycle and who never went without food or shelter, no matter where he found himself. Regardless of race, language, religion or culture, he was able to adapt his behaviours to those people he met in order first to avert any potential hostility, and then to enlist their positive support in matters of practical assistance. Such was his ability in this area that when we trained on an NLP practitioner course together, he was put to the task of helping me (I was not a natural at rapport-building) learn the same kinds of quick skills. On one occasion we were despatched to the West End of London for a rapport-building 'test'. We took it in turns to point to anyone we chose and our partner had to go up and create rapport with the chosen person or persons – we took pains to choose people as 'unlike' ourselves as possible. What was extraordinary was that in every case, regardless of race, age or overall differences in appearance, we were both able to create a powerful rapport using the matching technique *every time*. I learned once and for all that it is quite possible to go anywhere in the world and meet up with anyone and have within my control the potential to open up a positive relationship. I found this a thrilling realization, and am absolutely convinced it has been one of the foundation pieces in my career progress to date. For example, it has without doubt helped me to succeed in interviews, presentations, sales pitches and, of course, coaching.

For an idea of how my friend operates with people from different cultures you might look at some of Michael Palin's travel films for a comparison. Like my friend, Palin seems able to make a positive impact wherever he goes. True, this is sometimes just about being smiley and unthreatening (and no doubt to some extent the film crews pave the way in advance), but clearly it goes beyond that to conveying genuineness and trustworthiness – something of the three Rs in fact.

Matching needs to happen at more than one level: alongside technique comes the need for the right mental attitude and values system. Rapport is only a precursor of trust and confidence in a relationship, though a highly important one. As a coach there is no point in being technically skilled as a creator of rapport if your intention is *not* to convey acceptance and respect for your client. This in itself may need to be learned consciously to begin with – we do not always think in this saintly way about each other in our busy business lives, often almost automatically reverting to snap negative judgements on anybody who does not seem superficially to resemble us.

I have a trigger thought which I use before seeing each client, which is to imagine my 'highest self' about to greet someone else's 'highest self'. This seems to switch me on to being at my most open, receptive and respectful, no matter how fed up, tired or irritated by the frustrations of life I might be just before the coaching session. This is just one of the ways in which coaching others does *me* some good.

Congruence and rapport

The ideal state for coaching can best be described as *congruent:* feeling in alignment with oneself at all levels and extending that congruent alignment to one's view of the client. I find this congruence can be achieved in all sorts of ways, sometimes by my 'trigger' thoughts, sometimes by making sure I feel *physically* congruent by breathing deeply and centering the weight and balance of my body – after all, the mind and body is an interactive system and what happens in one part of the system affects the other parts too. Physical behaviours can affect beliefs and values just as much as beliefs can create behaviours. You can sometimes think yourself into new behaviours, but you can *also* behave your way into new thinking, and this is often a more direct, easier, process. Suppose, for example, that at some future point you find yourself in need of creating a little more confidence for yourself. There are numerous options open to you in the confidence-boosting line, derived both from NLP and from other sources. However, you can simply begin to *act* more confidently. Here is a simple exercise: imagine another version of yourself a few feet away looking fantastically confident in your physical being, and simply step into that version of you. Notice the positive difference – see the world from the eyes, hear the world from the ears, and just feel the physical confidence of this 'other' you. You will quickly notice how your thoughts change into a more positive, confident vein. If you want to, you could then step into an even *more* confident version of you.

Matching the physical behaviour of your client to some degree makes it easier for them not to set up some kind of unconscious resistance to you as a coach, particularly in the earliest stages of a relationship. This is particularly important at this sensitive early stage when the client may be feeling anxious about the situation. First impressions are notoriously lasting and powerful – anyone who has done any interviewing, for example, knows that it is hard not to make some kind of judgement about the interviewee in the very early *seconds* of the interview. And if this first impression is a negative one in any way, it is difficult for the interviewee to go on and correct it in the subsequent fifty-nine minutes.

I remember watching a boxing match on television once in which 'our boy' was knocked out in the first round. His manager explained to the commentator that the defeated boxer 'was much better in long fights'. This is a close analogy to the need to create rapport early in relationships – you might not get to know what a long-term relationship is like if you keep getting rejected at first sight.

Matching/mismatching exercise

If you would like to experience the power of physical matching, and the consequences of *mis*matching, try the following exercise with a willing friend or colleague:

- Sit in two chairs in the coaching position (i.e. not quite face to face but angled slightly away from each other to avoid any suggestion of confrontation).
- Match the body language of your partner as closely as possible while avoiding anything likely to induce humour or offence, like mimicking a nervous twitch.

- Ask your friend/colleague to talk to you for about a minute on a subject for which they have enthusiasm and which is to at least some extent important to them, e.g. a relationship, an interest/hobby, or perhaps something they are looking forward to. Explain that you are not going to respond to them verbally in the normal way but are going to match their physical behaviour only. Ask them to keep going for the full minute (timed by you), no matter what they see you doing.
- Explain before they begin that you will be deliberately mismatching them for a few seconds at roughly half way through the minute, but will return to matching their behaviour quickly.
- Ask them to begin talking, and match their physical presentation as closely as possible.
- After about half a minute, deliberately *mismatch* their behaviour. Make the mismatch a small one, something like looking at the clock for a few seconds, checking your watch, noticing you have a shoelace undone, glancing out of the window for a few seconds or just shifting your posture.
- After a few seconds of mismatching, go back into full matching mode until the minute is over, and when it seems OK to interrupt, ask your friend or colleague to finish what they are saying.

You can be prepared for a fairly strong, though almost certainly at least partly amused, response from your colleague. Ask them:

- how they felt about you and the relationship between you when you were matching their behaviour
- how they felt when you mismatched them
- what happened to their levels of concentration and focus when you mismatched
- how they responded to your behaviour at a values level
- what it was like for them when you returned to matching.

I have run this exercise in groups for many years and the reactions to the match/mismatch/match sequence are amazingly consistent. The persons doing the talking consistently report some or all of the following responses:

- an initial positive feeling about the relationship – based on a perception that they were being very closely listened to
- shocked or wrong-footed by the mismatch to the degree that many people feel they cannot continue
- complete or at least considerable loss of concentration and focus – a 'losing of the place'

- a perception of being strongly insulted
- often a loss of confidence in the relationship as they thought it had been.

Just to confirm the power of this exercise, get your friend/colleague to do the same for you. Even though you absolutely know the mismatch is coming you will almost certainly be thrown by it.

Among other things, this exercise causes many people to reflect upon how little they generally attempt to create rapport in their daily lives, and indeed how few people make the attempt to create rapport with them. For coaches this is an absolute must: if you need further motivation to master some rapport skills it might help you to know that people think better when they are feeling well listened to – so as a coach, creating rapport is in itself going to help your client make progress on their issues.

Matching is not mimicry

Sometimes students on our courses express concerns that matching amounts to mimicry – an expression of disrespect. They are right to have this concern, because nothing should be further from the intentions of the coach. It is critically important to get this right in your mind. One example might be how you feel about voice-matching on the telephone: some of our coaching students have mentioned this as an area that often seems to happen 'naturally', but where they are not really sure themselves whether they are matching or mimicking. They notice, perhaps, that their voice changes a little to take on aspects of a distinctive accent, or changes pace to move closer to the speed of the voice at the other end of the line, and wonder if they themselves are behaving inauthentically.

I firmly believe the key issue here is the quality of your *intention*. If you *intend* to convey respect by matching (which is an indication of your willingness to move towards someone else's model of the world), then the client, or other person, will pick up, even if unconsciously, your intention to respect them. If your intention is to manipulate or deceive then at an unconscious level at least your client or other person will pick this up too.

Matching and empathy

Another benefit of the deliberate matching process is the degree to which it helps the coach gain *empathy* with the client. By matching, I find I can determine a great deal about how the client is feeling, particularly with regard to energy and mood. I have sometimes been able to detect when the client is not feeling completely well – perhaps suffering back-pain or headache. You might try this for yourself. When meeting someone, match their behaviour as closely as possible and ask yourself what *they* are feeling like: if the relationship allows it, you might check out your perceptions with them to see how accurate they are. On one NLP course I attended we were asked to walk behind someone for several minutes while matching their behaviour as closely as possible, and it was a very powerful experience to have the sensation of 'being' someone else for a short while – the perceptions we were able to gather about how the other person was feeling and even thinking were sometimes uncanny. You could try sitting behind a colleague or friend and matching them – notice how much you learn about what it is like to be 'in their shoes' for a while.

At the very least, by doing this matching you will be putting your attention on the client rather than on yourself – and this alone helps to create the conditions of rapport.

Matching, pacing and leading

Another benefit of habitually matching your clients physically is that it allows you to tune in to their mood and energy, as noted above. This is a good thing in itself, but what if you then perceive the client to be in some kind of negative state unlikely to be conducive to good coaching? Clients frequently present themselves in such states – perhaps tired, low in energy, anxious or mildly depressed. Our common-sense approach tells us that what we need to offer as a remedy is the *opposite* state, but this can actually make things worse. As a frequently grumpy person myself, I know full well how irritating it can be to be 'cheered up', for example. The last thing I need when wallowing around in my dark thoughts is to be told perkily what a lovely day it is or be invited to count my blessings – these things tend to make me feel more committed to the mood I was already in. I have noticed too that my attempts to 'cheer up' colleagues with jokes or witticisms have more than once resulted in an abruptly closed door. Similarly, if a client is very low in energy or tired, the last thing they really need is for 'the dynamic coach' to spring into the room exhorting the benefits of good body posture and deep breathing allied to a positive mental attitude.

However, neither is it desirable for the coach to do nothing to shift the negative state of the client. Indeed if the coach does nothing, it is possible or even likely that they themselves will get caught up in the negativity and get dragged down by the client. In this state they can be of little use to the client and are in effect colluding with a non-resourceful state of mind. The NLP approach involves starting off where the client is, i.e. *matching* as described above. The next step is to go along with the client as they are being, for a short period. This is known as *pacing*, i.e. maintaining rapport over time.

The next step is *leading*. This is the step that needs most judgement and skill on the part of the coach. The idea is to move your own energy level or mood to a more resourceful state, and by so doing send a (primarily unconscious) message to your client that they too will need to move if they are to remain in rapport with you. If this is timed well, you will see the client shift posture and energy in a variety of different ways in response to the lead you are giving them.

I have found that different moods require different lengths of time spent on the pacing of rapport. In low-energy, downbeat clients I generally find it useful to stay with them for several minutes before shifting my posture and lifting my energy to something more 'upbeat'. With a client who is agitated, or even angry, I find I have to move through the gears more quickly. With anger I tend to match the energy, stance and volume of the client for just a few seconds – perhaps five seconds is all it needs – before softening and moderating my being to offer a model of something calmer and more controlled.

Some people may have concerns that this behaviour is, or could be, manipulative. Again, I would assert that the root issue is the intention behind the act: the technique itself has no ethical currency, either positive or negative. For decades there have been books published and seminars run on subjects such as assertiveness, 'winning friends and influencing people', getting ahead in business and so forth – the wish to manage relationships effectively has been present for a long time before NLP. At heart I believe people know if they are being manipulated and if the person they are engaged with is authentic or not. However, I also believe that it is important to operate as a coach within an explicit as well as implicit culture of ethical practice: Jenny Rogers lays out a useful ethical code in her book *Coaching Skills* which serves extremely well as a guide in this area.

Many people find the matching–pacing–leading approach to meeting anger counter-intuitive, and instinctively believe that anger should be met with pacifying and calming behaviour from the outset. I personally find it far more effective to use the matching–pacing–leading sequence, although I grant it does take a little bit of practice to get the timing right, and can even take a little bit of nerve at first. To develop your confidence, I would recommend the following:

- Practise with a friend or colleague – get them to role-play the behaviour you want to match, pace and lead, and get them to give you feedback on how effective your behaviour is being.
- In dealing with anger, confine yourself to *matching* the energy level of the other person – some people find it tempting at first to 'over-

match', i.e. try to outdo the level of anger. Build confidence in *immediately* matching the anger level for those few vital seconds before leading your client down to a calmer state. The content of what is being said is far less important than matching the energy, so there is no need to worry about getting the words precisely right.

- Take no risks! I would not recommend trying to match anyone who is physically threatening, disturbed, or out of control – confine this technique to behaviours within a sensible range.

Remember, too, that anger towards you as a coach is extremely rare, and that it can be cathartic for a client to display anger at times: as with most things in coaching, you have to make your own judgement.

Matching, pacing and leading in practice

I once coached a manager in the hospitality industry whose issue was the difficulty he had in managing someone he described as an 'archetypal tem-peramental chef'. This manager had wanted to discuss some changes he wanted the chef to make and the chef had interpreted the attempted dis-cussion as criticism. The chef's response was to go silent – to literally refuse to speak: apparently he (the chef) would sit with his legs spread out just staring at the ceiling. My client described how he had tried 'everything' to get the chef to talk – chiefly, as it transpired, threats, praise and promises. What became clear as he described these attempts was that he was operating at a very different level physically from the chef: he was in fact hugely out of rapport in terms of posture, energy, pace, facial expression, use of voice – the works. Though sceptical, my client agreed he would try to match the silent behaviour of the chef should it arise again. Indeed it did arise, and the two of them sat in silence for a very long-seeming (to my client) ten minute. Eventually my client could bear the tension no more and made a very small movement in preparation to speak but at that moment the chef turned his head, looked him in the eye and said 'OK, let's talk' – or similar words. They went on to have the discussion the manager had wanted in the first place.

A more dramatic intervention was the instance of the mild-mannered senior manager of a finance house. Terry was part of a senior triumvirate of equal status who managed the company under the chief executive. The problem was that Terry was being bullied by the other two very aggressive, highly competitive men. I had in fact met them and can confirm the truth of Terry's description of their behaviour. Terry's approach hitherto had been one of appeasement, but the more appeasing his behaviour was, the more aggressive the other two managers became. I asked Terry to role-play a recent occasion when he felt he had been bullied. He described to me an instance earlier in the week when one of the other managers had burst into his office. Terry described to me the behaviour of the other manager in detail and I took on his role. In character, I simulated bursting into Terry's office, banging my fist on his desk and demanding to know 'What the . . . . . had gone wrong with the . . . . . IT system!' Terry's response, even in the role-play, was astonishing – he virtually curled up in his chair and started whining and apologizing. His behaviour seemed actually to wind me up in the role I was playing – every excuse and whine seemed to make me more angry and aggressive.

I gave Terry feedback on how his behaviour was affecting me and we discussed the idea of his matching, pacing and leading some of the aggression of his colleagues. Terry agreed to replay the role play with me as preparation. I repeated my desk-thumping and swearing but before I had got as far as a second sentence, Terry jumped to his feet, banged *his* fist on the table and asked in a voice that mirrored mine in terms of volume and energy: 'What the . . . . do you think you are doing bursting into my office like that?' The effect on me was electric – even in role I felt stopped in my tracks, finding myself stumbling for apologetic and self-justifying phrases. Terry quite quickly lowered the volume and energy of his voice, and very soon we were talking at more or less the same level. After a little more coaching and practice Terry agreed he would try this behaviour out on his two colleagues. It worked, and what could have been a doomed set of relationships survived and improved. Interestingly, Terry reported back to me in a subsequent session that both of his colleagues had been worried about their own behaviours and the relationship with Terry. All three men felt relief when Terry stood up for himself: there was a sense of rebalancing in the relationship.

Matching metaphors and language patterns

Another highly effective way of creating rapport is to pay close attention to the specific words, metaphors and language patterns used by your clients. At the most basic level it is useful to mirror back to the clients, perhaps as part of a summary, some of the words they use, particularly the words they might express with the greatest emphasis. Some of the most significant words the client can offer the coach are the simple metaphors and similes they might use. These metaphors and similes offer the opportunity for the coach to try some matching, pacing and leading of a different sort, using language. For example:

CLIENT: When I think about the all the decisions I've got to make, it makes me feel as if I am coming up to a huge crossroads – more like Spaghetti Junction in fact!

COACH: And what does Spaghetti Junction feel like to you right now?

CLIENT: Well, it's really big and busy and confusing, and the traffic is coming up to it really fast – it feels like it's going to be difficult to slow down enough to judge which way I should go! I feel like I'm going into it out of control!

COACH: OK, so how about we slow down now and think about it? We could even sit in the lay-by for a while so you can make a few calm decisions well before you get there!

Matching key words, similes and metaphors lets the client know you are really listening, and really tuned in to their world as they are experiencing it in a given moment. Client and coach can play together with the metaphors to explore them for new meanings or understandings – perhaps even for the way forward on their issue.

For some clients, however, the metaphors they are using may actually be contributing to their issue. While a rich source of insight for the coach into how a client is thinking, metaphors can also reveal assumptions and limitations the client is putting onto their thinking about a given issue. Business leaders, like everyone else, are apt to reveal their thinking patterns about business issues via their use of metaphor:

CLIENT: I see the battle for supremacy in this marketplace being fought over the Pacific Rim countries – we've got to send our troops out there and scare the enemy off!

COACH: Wow – sounds like you think of your business as a war!

CLIENT: Well, it is *kind* of like a war – we certainly can't afford to be faint hearted, that's for sure. The troops have got to show guts.

COACH: So if business is war, who gets hurt?

CLIENT: Well, now you mention it, my team is getting kind of stressed out – and no one seems to laugh much at the moment.

COACH: So what might be a more useful metaphor for you to think about that would let your team put a lot of energy and commitment in but still have time for some fun?

CLIENT: Well, perhaps we could start thinking about it more as a competitive game – after all, no one really gets hurt...

In order to match, pace and lead metaphors, the coach needs to use very much the same process as with the physical behaviours described above. First the coach *matches* the metaphor by mirroring it back, then *paces* it by exploring it with the client, and finally *leads* it by exploring more positive alternatives.

Language and sensory systems

One of the early contributions of NLP to the subject of rapport was the research linking language to the sensory experience of individuals. This was a very important development in challenging common-sense assumptions about how we experience and create our personal worlds. In a nutshell, the language you use both *reflects* and *creates* internal sensory states. Someone who, for example, uses a lot of visual words and expressions is highly likely to be experiencing their world in a predominantly visual way: someone who uses a lot of auditory words and phrases is likely to be experiencing their world in a primarily auditory way, and so on. The common-sense view is different, a default assumption that we all experience the world in more or less the same way.

The implications for rapport are significant: someone who primarily 'sees' their world is likely have a different experience from someone who 'feels' it (in either the tactile or emotional sense of the word) or 'hears' it.

Here is how people with different habits in this area might describe, let's say, the future of their organization. Someone with a visual preference might say: 'When I look to the future, I see a vision of success. Coming over the horizon is a dazzling vista of opportunity. It really looks to me as if we are at last starting to see the way ahead.' Someone with an auditory preference might say: 'The future is calling out, and it is ringing a bell of hope. We need to create a call to arms and get everyone singing from the same hymn sheet.' Someone with a kinaesthetic (either feeling in the emotional sense or in the physical sense of touching) might say: 'The future is rock solid – I really feel this. We have got to get a grip on our opportunities and anchor ourselves to our course. With hope in our hearts we can press on.'

Bear in mind too that there are also the important senses of taste and smell. In human beings these seem to be of lesser importance to most people most of the time but there are still occasions when they have important significance and when they appear in speech. I have a friend whose olfactory (smell) and gustatory (taste) senses seem very developed and important to him. His language would be 'peppered' with words like spicy, piquant, tasty, raw and pungent. Perhaps not surprisingly food and its attendant joys and temptations are very much part of his life.

Any book on basic NLP will provide chapter and verse on this subject. Overall I have found it useful in coaching to look for *patterns* in the way clients seem to experience the world rather than put too much trust in very specific observations. With practice you will begin to notice the habituations people have in this area – whether they are *primarily* visual, auditory, kinaesthetic, or even olfactory/gustatory. A good starting point would be to check out your *own* patterns. You will begin to notice the kinds of words you use and how they relate to your internal sensory experience: whether in fact you tend to be visualizing, listening or feeling.

Language and eye movements

NLP has established a degree of connection between a person's eye movements, how they are experiencing the world internally and how this experience is reflected in their language. Learning how to make sense of the eye movements of ourselves and others gives rich insight into how we/they are processing information internally. Recognizing eye movements and the patterns that individuals create does take practice, because the pace at which people make these movements varies from quite slow and deliberate to brief subtle 'flicks' of the eyes.

This is how it is organized: if you imagine looking at someone's face you can divide it mentally into upper, middle and lower zones (see Figure 3.1). The upper zone is where people *tend* to look if they are thinking visually – making pictures. The middle zone, specifically with eye movements to the left or right, is where the eyes tend to move when people are processing sound. The lower zone is the area where the eyes tend to move when someone is involved with their feelings or talking to themselves. There are some important differences in left- and right-sided movements too: for right-handed people, looking to the left generally equates with the past, e.g. remembered images and sounds, and looking to the right equates to future or imagined images and sounds.

When coaching, you can learn to spot the patterns in client thinking – for example, someone who constantly looks upwards when speaking is very likely to be doing a certain amount of visualizing. By noticing their predominant eye movements and their accompanying language, you can create an idea of *how* they are thinking (but of course *what* they are thinking is for them to reveal only as they choose: NLP does not offer mind-reading capabilities). The benefits of this pattern recognition to rapport-building are great: as a coach you can extend the matching process to this detailed and important aspect of behaviour. You can also apply the matching/pacing/leading sequence to eye movements and language patterns in order to bring new perspectives and different resource states to the client. For example, I once had a client who tended to get stuck in 'problem' mode from time to time: when this happened he would habitually drop his eyes to the floor for long periods. Once I had spotted the pattern I was able to encourage him to lift his eyes upwards and change his focus to what he *wanted* in relation to his issue, i.e. to get him outcome-focused in his thinking and in his *way* of thinking.

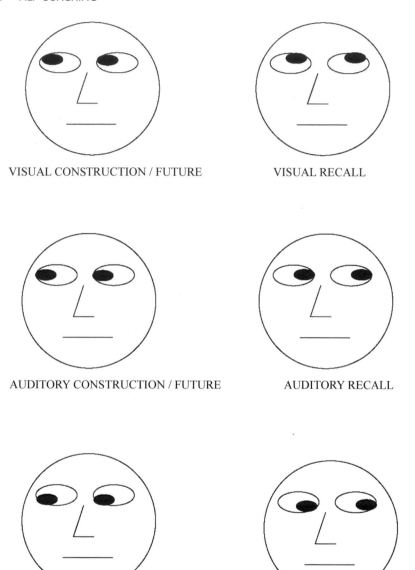

VISUAL CONSTRUCTION / FUTURE VISUAL RECALL

AUDITORY CONSTRUCTION / FUTURE AUDITORY RECALL

TOUCH / TASTE / SMELL
FEELINGS / EMOTIONS

SELF TALK / INTERNAL DIALOG

Figure 3.1

Build flexibility

It is important not to stereotype yourself and others in this area – it is wrong to label people as 'being' visual, auditory or kinaesthetic. Neither is it the case that any particular sensory patterns are better than any other. The point is that 'what you don't use, you lose' – if you habitually do not use parts of your sensory apparatus, you tend to place restrictions on the range of thinking and feeling that is available to you. The preferences people exhibit are not absolute restrictions, just habits, and we all have the potential to change habits if we choose. I learned during my NLP training that I had a heavy auditory dominance – to this day if I walk into a room or a building I tend to be more affected by its sound qualities than by anything else, including the furnishings or colour scheme. But I have learned over time that there is a whole world of other experiences out there – that I can change or even enhance the quality of my experience by paying more attention to different parts of it. I have taught myself to be more visual and kinaesthetic when I choose to be, with liberating and energizing results. I achieved this by developing the habit of noticing when I was in a particular sensory 'mode' in my head, and by consciously making a change if I chose. For example, I might be thinking ahead to a forthcoming event, say a party, and recognize that what I was doing was planning lots of conversations in my head: by switching consciously to 'visual' mode – making imaginary pictures – I was also able to enjoy anticipating what things would *look* like, something that gave me an enriched representation of what was ahead, and a greater sense of anticipatory pleasure.

   I have also been able to work with clients from time to time in making them more conscious of how they appear to be experiencing the world. I remember in particular one client who found it a revelation that he could *choose* to see lots more pictures in his head: this was an important change from his predominant habit of working with sounds and feelings, and led to more flexibility – and potential resourcefulness – of thinking.

Sensory systems and mood

By developing your flexibility in experiencing the world through your senses you can enhance your resourcefulness and flexibility. As a very small example of this, try the following. Sit with your head level, and move your eyes upwards as far as they will go. Notice your mood with your eyes at this level, and then gradually, slowly, move your eyes downwards while keeping your head level. Notice how your mood changes as your eyes move slowly downwards – most people report that their mood becomes more serious and even sombre as their eyes track downwards, and becomes 'lighter' when they move their eyes back upwards.

Language and its impact on rapport in coaching

Sheila was a highly skilled NHS chief executive who found herself in a somewhat uneasy relationship with her Trust's chairperson. The surface relationship seemed good enough – there was a civil, cooperative, constructive tone – but underneath it she felt that real understanding and rapport were missing. At times it seemed to her that they were speaking different languages. This led her to feel she was not really trusted by her chairperson and that as a result she, the chairperson, was too 'hands on', not leaving Sheila to get on with the job. This relationship was critically important to Sheila – without it going well her leadership of the Trust would be significantly weakened. Sheila wanted to use her coaching to make the relationship with her chairperson more trusting and robust so they could talk more freely and get to issues quicker and with greater understanding.

Eventually Sheila and the chairperson agreed we should work as a trio and look at the relationship, with me acting as coach to both. There followed a number of meetings with them, both together and individually. As we explored the relationship it became apparent that, despite a basic wish to cooperate and a high level of civility, there was a relatively low degree of rapport. Although both claimed to respect each other they seemed a little uneasy when talking together and over-careful in the way they would choose their words, as if anxious not to make a mistake or cause offence. At the root of this unease was a lack of basic rapport. When I listened to them speaking together, it became obvious to me they were talking almost different languages: Sheila's was peppered with visual words and her chairperson's with 'feelings' words, of both emotional and kinaesthetic types. Sheila would talk about her 'vision' for the organization, while her chair found it 'hard to get a handle' on what she was saying. It required a short crash course in getting both parties aware of how they each were representing the world to themselves to make a communications breakthrough which, ultimately, released the relationship into much greater freedom and understanding. They were initially a little perplexed by the concept of sensory bias in language, but they quickly took to the concept and began to make adjustments for each other – they developed a literal degree of 'common sense'. In fact, the process of learning about this aspect of themselves and each other in itself strengthened their rapport.

In summary, rapport-building in all its many possible forms is the absolute foundation of the coaching relationship. NLP is an important source of ideas and techniques for creating and maintaining this rapport, and thus in helping a client be at their most resourceful when being coached – and beyond.

4 Relationships and the meta-mirror

A very high proportion of the coaching clients with whom I work have issues around their working relationships. Indeed I would suggest that the majority of the coaching assignments I have undertaken over the years have involved relationship issues of one sort or another. In the world of work, the ability to create and maintain positive relationships is absolutely at the heart of effective working – the research on emotional intelligence suggests it is perhaps *the* critical factor in achieving career success, given an acceptable level of technical competence. The subject area from the coaching point of view is enormous: managing your boss, working with colleagues, leading teams, settling into a new role, working in business partnerships – the list is virtually endless. Here is just a tiny sample of some of the relationship issues that have come my way:

- needing to stand up for oneself – saying 'no' or asking for one's rights
- fear of someone else at work
- worries that a relationship has got stuck or is deterioraratng
- needing to be more persuasive
- needing to influence or negotiate more effectively in a range of contexts
- needing to manage difficult meetings.

Bear in mind that predominantly I have been coaching organizational *leaders:* each of these leaders was highly intelligent, experienced and able. They generally would have very strong intellectual abilities and a clear strategic grasp of what they were trying to achieve for their organization, but were to at least some extent frustrated or even stymied by issues of relationship and communication.

A note on the assertiveness approach

In his book *Using Your Brain – For a Change*, (1979) NLP pioneer Richard Bandler suggests in a sarcastic way that 'assertiveness training' should really be called 'loneliness preparation'. This is perhaps a little savage, but he does have a point. When I was trained as a social worker in the early 1980s we were drilled in assertiveness techniques as the basic method for effective communication and influence. The intention was positive – to master a mode of effective communication based on the principle of mutual respect, for oneself and for the other person in the relationship. Using assertiveness techniques you would in theory be able to get what you felt was your entitlement while respecting the legitimate needs of others.

The general problem with much assertiveness training was that it lacked an underlying active principle of *flexibility*. The language of assertiveness became tainted, fairly or unfairly, with perceptions of rigid, 'politically correct' phraseology: 'I hear what you're saying', 'Let's look for a win–win solution' and the classic 'With respect . . .' were regarded by many people as pretentious, predictable and clichéd.

Bandler also pointed out that assertiveness techniques only worked where both parties were sharing something of the same paradigms of values and behaviour. In some of the mean streets of American cities, he pointed out, where 'you could get killed for a ham sandwich', practising assertiveness techniques would get you into big trouble. Even in the relatively benign and homogeneous realm of business or organizational life, no two people share *exactly* the same paradigm or world view: therefore the skilled communicator/ influencer needs to be able to adopt a highly flexible approach in order to be effective – while at the same time maintaining a congruent hold on their own identity and values. It was from these assumptions that many of the rapport and communication techniques of NLP arose.

Offering advice

The temptation to offer advice in relationship issues is as great as, if not greater than, it is in other areas of coaching. However, the way forward for the client has to come from the client themselves in this area. And the way forward is rarely about logic or knowledge. Clients often know what they *should* do – the reason they often do not *do* what they know they should do is generally not an intellectual issue, but an emotional one, or a matter of perception. To offer an obvious example: it would be pointless as a coach to work with a client to confront a bully and to look at the techniques for doing this effectively if the real issue is the client's fear.

NLP approaches to relationship issues in coaching

NLP offers the coach many tools to allow a client to discover or rediscover resources needed to make progress on their relationship issues.

A characteristic of the NLP approach is its flexibility: tools described in other chapters as being helpful in working with other issues might be equally helpful or appropriate in the context of relationship work.

Working with *well-formed outcomes*, for example, might be an entirely appropriate way to help a client start thinking about their issue – some relationship issues are problematic precisely *because* the client is unclear about what they actually *want* from the relationship. I clearly recall working with a business leader who was deeply frustrated with his executive team, just as they were equally frustrated with him. The root of the mutual frustration was that, although the leader had very high expectations of the team, it was not clear in his mind exactly how these expectations should be met in their behaviour. He did not have, or express, sufficient clarity in his mind about the actual behaviour he was looking for from them. He tended to talk to them in high-level conceptual language about such things as 'taking initiative' or 'breaking the mould', and neither he nor they were able to understand what he really wanted. By using the well-formed outcomes process we were able to give him, and subsequently the team, much greater clarity. Specifically I was able to focus him on the *evidence* he was looking for in the behaviour he wanted, in direct sensory terms – i.e. what he wanted to *see, hear and feel* in terms of their behaviour. When he was able to say directly what he wanted, the team knew where they stood and were able to go about satisfying his requests.

Working with *self-limiting beliefs* is another useful approach. Clients frequently get stuck or become dissatisfied in their relationships at work (and in their private lives for that matter) because they carry assumptions or beliefs about what they can/cannot or should/should not do. One rather poignant example was a woman I coached who had risen to executive status on the basis of hard work and intellectual ability, but who, despite generally good self-esteem, found it very difficult to ask for what she needed for herself in the work context – she could not even bring herself to claim her business expenses. We worked on this and eventually it emerged that she had a deep-seated belief that it was 'wrong' to ask for things for yourself – a belief established in early childhood as the consequence of a combination of parental and school ethos. We were able to install a much more empowering belief using the self-limiting beliefs framework. She was able to bring this to bear in many of her working relationships.

As a coach, you will need to create and maintain positive relationships with your various clients, and be able to help them to do the same in their relationships both inside and outside the workplace. To do this you will need to understand and work with the concept and practice of *rapport-building*. Indeed the ability to create rapport with oneself and then with others is at the heart of successful relationships (see Chapter 3).

In this chapter I will focus specifically on the 'perceptual positions' or 'meta-mirror' technique, a 'set piece' from NLP that has helped many thousands of people over many years to review and renew the way they relate to the people who are important to them.

The 'perceptual positions' or 'meta-mirror' technique

I first learned this technique in 1988 on my practitioner training. At the time I initially found it so radically different from anything else I had experienced that I was suspicious of it – if this wasn't evidence of NLP as a load of Californian mumbo-jumbo, what was? I did not realize at the time that the technique was drawn and adapted from a lengthy and respectable tradition of what is called 'two-chair work' in Gestalt therapy.

To this day I often feel I need to pave the way carefully in preparing clients to try the technique for themselves. The key reason for this caution and carefulness of approach is that the technique is very powerful and effective – it works, and it works quickly. This in itself can be challenging to the expectations of many clients: many of us are not used to the concept of quick, powerful, positive change, having habituated to the belief that any positive change (if realizable at all) needs to be the result of slow, persistent effort of the 'no pain, no gain' variety.

It can be challenging to many of us to find that pleasant, desirable change can be achieved quickly and with lasting effect. Paradoxically, we often seem happy to accept the reality of *negative* change being quick and lasting: something bad happens to us and we think it is for ever. I have lost count of the number of times, for example when looking at self-limiting beliefs, that a client experiences something in their youth, say an episode of failure or rejection, and generalizes from this single event that they are 'failures' or 'unlovable' for ever. The power of the technique means that it needs to be introduced to the client with due care and respect for the maintenance of rapport.

This technique can be used when a client has identified a relationship they wish to improve in some way. This does not necessarily mean a problematic relationship, although in practice this seems to be the case in most coaching scenarios. It is worth emphasizing that knowledge and use of the technique can help someone to get the very best out of their most cherished relationships, ones that are already going well – I have seen many clients who fill up with love and pride as they work through the technique in order to improve already wonderful relationships, perhaps with their children or partners.

The crux of the technique sits elegantly at the heart of the principles of both coaching and NLP: it is directly focused on helping someone access their resourcefulness and, in so doing, to effect desired change. It also challenges the assumption we can fall into that somehow 'a relationship' is a static and tangible thing: instead, relationships are redefined as active, dynamic and open to influence and improvement by changes in behaviour.

To change someone else, first change yourself

One of the most significant aspects of the meta-mirror technique is that it focuses the responsibility for change in a relationship on the clients themselves rather than on the other people in the relationships they wish to improve. Very often clients want to change the other person – or at least they complain about how the other person in the relationship is behaving towards *them*. The meta-mirror focuses clients on what *they* themselves can do to make an improvement in a relationship and on helping them to access the personal resources they need in order to make positive changes in their own attitudes and behaviours.

How it works

Let me describe the technique and then look at a couple of real examples of how it has worked so well in coaching. I have seen numerous variations on this technique, and offer a slightly personalized format that works very well for me and for the majority of students of coaching to whom I teach it. I outline a quite detailed account of my approach because I think the details are particularly important in facilitating the client's process effectively and safely.

It is particularly important that you stick only to the questions and steps I describe here: sometimes the urge to get involved in understanding the content is strong, leading the coach into the temptation to ask extra questions of a counselling nature, e.g. questions beginning with 'why?' You should avoid this temptation if the client is to get full benefit.

Having helped the client to identify the relationship they want to improve and explained the reasons for using the technique, take the client through the following steps.

Step 1

Have the client sit down, and sit down or kneel next to them, side by side (in the interest of maintaining rapport). Ask the client to imagine the 'other person' sitting in an (actual) chair placed opposite them (see Figure 4.1). Encourage the client to create as complete a visual image as possible, and check they have done this. Ask the client for some way of referring to the imaginary person, but leave open to the client the right to use a made-up name or perhaps a single initial if they are at all sensitive about a confidentiality issue – the whole exercise, as with all coaching, should be about facilitating *process* rather than trying to understand or interpret *content*.

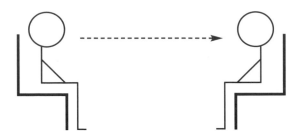

Figure 4.1

Ask the client how they *feel* when they look at the imaginary person. Be aware that many clients will respond to a 'feeling' question with a 'thinking' answer. If they do this, persist in asking for a genuine 'feeling' word. Repeat the question, 'How do you feel when you look at X?' several times, until the client runs out of answers – this is almost always after they have identified three, four or five feelings. Be aware that sometimes the feelings might be mixed: it is common for the feelings described to consist of mixtures like 'affection, admiration, anger and frustration'. It is useful to reflect back to the client the actual words they have chosen: this serves to let them know you are paying close attention and also allows them to reflect on what they have said – to check if these are indeed the feelings they have.

Step 2
Ask the client to stand, and stand up with them in order to maintain rapport. Suggest they breathe a little bit and perhaps 'shake out' as with a mild exercise routine: this is to ensure they are able to 'shake off' a particular state of mind and feeling.

Ask them to sit in the second chair, and sit or kneel next to them. Ask the client to imagine they *are* now the other person, this 'person X', and get them to imagine that *as* 'person X' they are looking back at themselves (the client) in the original chair (see Figure 4.2).

As before, give them the chance to create a strong visual image. Ask the question, 'As X, when you look back at yourself, how do you, *as X*, feel?' Again, make sure the response is one of feeling, not thinking. In particular, check that your client does not say something like 'I think X would feel ...' – make sure they use the words 'As X, I feel ...'. As in the first step, check that you have allowed them to express all their feelings – again, between three and five is typical.

At this point, as a result of metaphorically standing in the shoes of the 'other person', the client may begin to gain almost immediate insight into what they need to do to improve the relationship. Seeing the situation, even

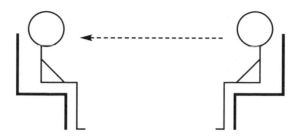

Figure 4.2

imaginarily, from the other person's point of view allows the client to develop empathy for the other person, resulting in new insight.

On the other hand, some clients can become a little concerned at this point, often because they are worried that any 'insight' they may have developed is the result of 'dubious' information, i.e. their 'mind-reading' of the other person while in the second position. You can reassure the client here that there is no mind-reading going on: the point of moving to the second person's position is to gain empathy and to bring to the forefront intuitive or instinctive thoughts and feelings about how the other person might be experiencing the relationship.

Step 3

Next, take the client to a position where they have an easy overview of the two chairs – usually several feet away, standing as the third point of a triangle between the chairs. After a brief 'shake-out', ask the client to take in the picture, i.e. create an imaginary 'tableau', with their imaginary self in the first chair and the other person in the second chair (see Figure 4.3).

This is the part of the technique where often the client really begins to benefit from seeing the relationship, literally, from different perspectives. The coach's job now is to help the client benefit from this new perspective by asking questions that help them to consolidate their learning. I favour sticking to the following few questions:

- How does the relationship strike you from this position?
- What do you want for the relationship?
- What will happen if nothing changes?
- What advice would you offer, from this position, to the 'you' sat in the first chair?

At this point, you as coach may notice some physical changes in the client: often they are more relaxed, and their voices sound more confident: breathing can be slower. I find I can increase this tendency for the client to

Figure 4.3

relax by 'leading' them with my own physicality, i.e. becoming more relaxed myself; and that so doing helps their concentration on the exercise.

Step 4
When you have finished asking the questions outlined in step 3, take the client to a fourth position where they can clearly see the two previous 'versions' of themselves, i.e. themselves in position 1 and 3 (see Figure 4.4). (It does not matter if they have a clear view of position 2 at this stage.)

After a very brief shake-out, let your client know two things: first, that this is getting close to the end of the exercise (they may be beginning to wonder by now), and second, that this is the key stage, where they will learn what resources they need to make use of to get what they want from the relationship. Ask them to focus visually on the two previous 'selves', i.e. the self in the first seat and the self standing in the third position. You can tell them to ignore the 'other person' for the time being! Get them to really visualize the two 'selves' and ask the following question: 'What resources does the *detached "you"* have that the *"you"* currently engaged in the relationship needs?'

Actually, this is the fancy way of asking the question. Depending on what considerations of rapport require, and using appropriate pointing, you could ask the question in other ways, such as: 'What has she/he got that she/he needs in that relationship?' The key is to ask the question that allows the

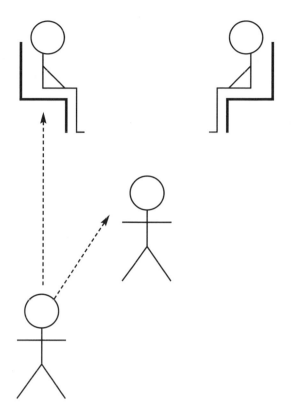

Figure 4.4

client to recognize the extra resourcefulness that the detached version of them has.

At an absolute minimum the client will notice the positive effect of the detachment itself, and how it allows them to take a cooler, more thoughtful overview, less crowded by their immediate emotions as experienced in the first position. In addition, clients frequently notice the 'detached' self has some or all of the following:

- more insight
- greater maturity (some clients even say their detached self *looks* more mature)
- greater wisdom
- more compassion
- a much clearer focus forwards.

And many more...

Final steps: making it count

The ultimate aim of the exercise is to put the client in touch with, and give them access to, their fullest resources in the context of the relationship. For this to happen the client needs to be able to go back to the original position and re-experience the relationship but *with all the resources they identified from their observations of the 'detached' self available to them*. There are several variations on how the coach takes them back to this position but I particularly like to do it in the following way.

Still in the fourth position, get the client to repeat to themselves all of the resources they notice in themselves in the detached or third position. Explain to them that you are going to take them back to this third position in order that they can 'take on' those resources. Take them back to the third position and invite them to feel and fully experience the resourcefulness they have in that position: for example, if they noticed from the fourth position that their detached self had more compassion, invite them to really feel the compassion back in the third position.

When the client is feeling fully 'resourced up', take them back to the first chair and ask them to have another look at the other person in the relationship now that they are in possession of their fullest resources. Ask them what they feel *now* when they look at the other person. There will be big differences, almost always totally positive. Most clients report back tremendous improvements in how they feel and much greater clarity about how to take the relationship forwards in the way they would want.

For an added touch, you could ask the client to sit once again, in the second position, as the other person in the relationship, and ask them *as* the other person (repeating step 2) to say how they feel looking back at themselves in the newly resourced state. The benefit of doing this is that invariably the 'other person' feels better as well as a result of the gains made by the client.

Summary of the technique

This is such a powerful and elegant technique that a book could be devoted to it alone. Over years of using it I have had almost exclusively positive results. Sometimes it happens that the client can get to the third position and recognize, in response to the question 'What do you *want* for the relationship?', that what they really want is for it to be over and done with. This can be a powerful moment for the client, and occasionally a few tears might result, but overwhelmingly they eventually recognize that to be free of a relationship that is no longer serving either party any useful purpose is a very positive thing.

Two examples from practice

Sandy

Sandy was a talented and experienced BBC department head who had made a significant achievement in combining two departments together to work in a more streamlined and cohesive way. He had created a new senior editorial team to run the new combined department, but was having trouble managing his relationship with one of the team. Sandy described this team member as a 'smiling assassin': he would appear to be all sweetness and light but at crucial and often highly public moments would attack (while still smiling) an important aspect of Sandy's leadership – typically a difficult decision he had made or a policy he was pursuing. Sandy wanted the assassin on board – he needed his talents – but was not prepared to tolerate the behaviour. The challenge Sandy wanted to address in coaching was how to get the behaviour he needed from this man without resorting to heavy-handed management tactics such as issuing ultimatums or going down a disciplinary route.

In position one, Sandy described his feelings as anger, fear, admiration and compassion. He was surprised to notice how mixed his feelings were, and even more surprised to note that deep down he was worried for this other man's wellbeing – he realized the other man was putting his immediate career prospects at risk by his behaviour and was 'painting himself into a corner'.

In position two, Sandy described the other man's feelings as anger, fear, admiration, jealousy and contempt. Sandy was struck by how some of the feelings mirrored his own (something that occurs more often than not in the meta-mirror). He was also struck by how strong the feeling of contempt was.

In the third position Sandy recognized that the relationship was heading for a severe crisis if the dynamic did not change. He realized that what he wanted for it was more openness about feelings and a mutual growth in trust, respect and honesty. The critical realization was that he, Sandy, would need to take the initiative and change his behaviour. Specifically he would need to be absolutely open about his negative feelings, say clearly what he wanted from the other man in terms of *his* behaviour and, finally, spell out the long-term consequences if this change of behaviour was not forthcoming. In short, he recognized the need to be honest, open and clear and to spell out how he saw things and what he expected in the future.

In the fourth position Sandy was amazed to note the comparison between the two different versions of himself in positions one and three. The resources he noticed in position three included clarity, perspective and personal strength – he was particularly taken with the latter, noting that in position three he looked and sounded like the leader he needed and wanted to be.

An interesting observation from Sandy was that in position three he seemed to himself to be about thirty years older than in position one – not in physical terms but in emotional terms. He perceived himself in position three to have retaken possession of all the hard-won experience and maturity that had somehow absented itself from his grasp in the context of the troublesome relationship. I was able to tell him that this often seemed to be the case in this particular exercise, i.e. that somehow people would seem to revert, psychologically speaking, to a less resourceful time of their lives in the context of a troubling relationship.

I told him of my experience with a mature and rather formidable businesswoman with whom I had once worked, who was having difficulty getting fair and respectful treatment from her large, loud, male boss, of whom she was frightened. She had noticed that in position three she was at least forty years older emotionally than in position one, where she felt like she had done when she was a little girl being told off by her large, loud father.

Sandy's realization was yet another example of the principle that the client is a resourceful being, and that it is only the change of context that might temporarily create a distance from a particular resource.

I took Sandy back to position three to reassociate himself with his mature, strong and resourceful self and then invited him to return to his original position. Back in position one Sandy noticed that his feelings, and indeed some of his literal perception of the other person, had changed. In place of anger and fear he had clarity of focus and a resolve to put the relationship on a positive footing. I invited him to take up the other person's position one last time, and Sandy was gratified to note that as the 'other person' he had gained respect for Sandy but had lost his fear, jealousy and contempt.

In reviewing the exercise I reminded Sandy that he had not been in a mind-reading exercise in position two but had been engaging and exploring his own intuitive and empathic feelings about the other person. We finished this part of the coaching session by looking at how Sandy was going to deal with the relationship back in the reality of the workplace. Sandy left the session confident that he was going to deal with it positively. The outcome as I last heard it from Sandy was that the 'smiling assassin' was now behaving much better and that a huge source of tension had been removed from the team.

I have continued to work intermittently with Sandy and it is interesting to reflect how a single exercise involving a change of perception and a reclaiming of emotional strength for one individual has had many powerful knock-on effects. His authority and respect within the team has grown as a result of the way in which he handled the 'assassin' (whose own career has been stabilized). The team in turn has gained confidence and purpose, and the effect on the wider department has been a tangible lift in morale and performance.

Karen

Karen was a local authority finance director whose team was under-performing: she felt she had tried everything to motivate the team but was not getting the response she had hoped for. Again, she wanted to avoid going down the 'heavy' route of disciplining members of the team – she felt they had the talent and ability needed but were just not getting the message about what she wanted from them in terms of performance. Karen could not understand how they could fail to understand her. She thought she had expressed her opinion and her requirements with unambiguous clarity – somehow it was falling on deaf ears, the team not seeming to respond with any sense of urgency or even with any grasp of what she was asking of them.

In this case the exercise revealed to Karen that she was simply not creating enough impact in how she was approaching the team. She learned that she had to express far more emotion – spell out specifically how angry and frustrated she was, albeit in a controlled way. The exercise itself contained a slight variation, as there was a whole team of people involved rather than an individual. I helped Karen to imagine a number of the team sitting in the second position. From this position she was able to recognize that her steady, measured approach to communication was obscuring her real feelings – that the team simply did not recognize how furious she was inside because she spoke with such calmness and apparent equanimity.

This insight gave Karen the impetus to change her communication style radically. However, for her to return to the team and express real emotion we had to do a supplementary piece of work on a *self-limiting belief* (see a full account on how to do this in Chapter 6) which was that it was 'wrong' to express anger. We also did a piece of role-play, giving her the chance to practise and get feedback from me on the impact of her communication. When we had worked through this, Karen had in place all the resources she needed to make her desired change – insight, motivation, skills and belief.

The meta-mirror as an aid to influence in group situations

Brian

Top leaders are frequently called upon to be influential in groups. Brian, an outstandingly talented NHS chief executive, was deeply troubled when it came to presenting an argument or a report to groups of senior managers and non-executive directors. There was a particular monthly meeting that filled him with so much dread that he had on two occasions literally fainted while preparing to speak. Brian felt that his career was in danger of stalling and was experiencing a severe level of distress and embarrassment over the issue. While treading carefully and being at pains to point out I was not in the business of attempting phobia cures, I did offer to try to help Brian with some of the techniques and tools drawn from coaching.

We went through a number of relatively conventional techniques including breathing, relaxation and visualization, but with little real benefit to Brian: eventually I decided to try the meta-mirror approach.

The approach is essentially the same as above, but with subtle differer-ences of wording. When he was in position one I asked Brian, 'How do you feel when you look at the group?'

Instead of taking the second-position viewpoint of the 'other person', one takes the viewpoint of the 'other persons'. I said something like, 'Imagine you are part of the group watching Brian prepare to speak. When you look at him, as part of the group, how do you feel?' It was this position that created the breakthrough learning for Brian: he recognized that the group was not, as he had assumed, conspiring to create his discomfort but was a group of individuals who wanted him to succeed and were terrified of their own embarrassment if he were to struggle to perform well in front of them.

In the third position I asked Brian to imagine he was standing to one side watching the whole scenario, and watched him relax visibly as he realized that the whole situation could, indeed *should*, be a win–win scenario. In the fourth position he was able to spot all the resources he needed, and actually possessed, to influence a group effectively.

The meta-mirror and stage fright

Kate

In another situation I was able to coach Kate, an actor whom our company employs as a professional role-player on our courses. Kate had grown scared to go onto an actual stage and perform in an actual drama – she had experienced bad dreams about forgetting her lines and was frightened of the audience. In this particular case I got her to imagine that in position one she *was* on stage: her description of her feelings when she looked at the audience included words like 'terrified', 'paralysed' and 'empty'. I then asked her to imagine herself in position two – imagining herself as part of the audience looking at the 'Kate' who was onstage. From this position she described her feelings as 'embarrassed', 'uncomfortable' or 'awkward' and worried. This insight was in itself useful to Kate – she had hitherto assumed the audience would be at least to a degree hostile: it was a relief to realize that the audience basically wanted her to succeed.

For the third position I asked Kate to imagine herself in the wings of the theatre. From this position she realized that she wanted to build on the positive feelings of the audience – to give them what they wanted from her as a performer. She was also able to give herself some advice about managing her nerves, building on all her years of experience and training: she in fact knew everything she was supposed to do to manage her nerves and confidence issues.

Finally we went to a fourth position, in the imaginary auditorium. From this position Kate was able to see that the version of herself in the wings was an experienced, capable, highly trained actor who had only been held back by her assumptions of audience hostility. Finally, we took her back through the positions and brought her resourceful self back to position one.

Variations and adaptations

Sometimes there is no need to go through the whole routine. I have on numerous occasions got to the third position and asked the client what they wanted from the relationship, only to hear them say something along the lines that what they most wanted was for the relationship to end, because they had had enough of it. This is by no means a negative outcome for the client – I can recall no occasion when this realization on their part had a negative impact, although sometimes there has been a degree of sadness at the thought of letting a relationship go. In general, there has been a sense of relief for the client when they understand they have the choice open to them to stop wasting their time, energy and emotional commitment on a dead-end relationship.

Another 'quick and dirty' variation in general coaching is to ask the client just to leave their chair and look at 'themselves' from a different position. From the different position you can ask them to think about what advice they might offer to the 'self' still in the chair. This can work very effectively as a stimulus to a client who may be feeling a bit blocked or stuck at a given moment in a session. It also changes the energy, generally giving the client something of a boost to their energy levels.

5 Building confidence and positive resource states

There is relatively little written in NLP literature about confidence as an explicit, separate subject. This to me is surprising, as confidence seems to be at the heart of so many issues brought by the coaching clients I see – my colleague coaches report similar experiences. It is sometimes true that confidence is subsumed as a subject under the general heading of 'resourcefulness' or 'resource states' in the NLP literature. There is no doubt that numerous NLP approaches and techniques can and do help to *create* confidence, but nonetheless it seems to me that coaches are so frequently dealing with specific confidence issues in their clients that it needs attention on its own as a subject. Perhaps with an eye for this gap in the market, Paul McKenna brought out in 2006 a self-help book called *Instant Confidence*. This book is an excellent, well-organized collection of techniques offered in simple language. It is also in itself a confident piece of work, modelling the state of confidence it asserts is possible for the reader to acquire. McKenna does not go in for lots of explanation as to why the techniques work – he simply asserts that they do, basing his assertions on his own long experience and learning. Indeed, so unwedded is he to the need for lots of intellectual justifications for the book's approach that he writes in bold at the beginning: 'You don't have to believe a single word I say.' His point is that most of the issues relating to confidence are to do with the unconscious mind – its initial programming via early experiences, and early responses to these experiences, that become the template for our basic assumptions about our selves and our lives. His book is a comprehensive programme designed to reprogramme the unconscious mind. I have no doubt the techniques in his book are highly effective. I have been using many of them, or slight variations of them, for years, both for my own benefit and in coaching.

However, in executive coaching you sometimes have to win the intellectual argument – you have to be able to explain, sometimes in detail, why you would like to try a particular technique or approach with a client. In effect, you have to create a sense of confidence in the conscious mind of your client to allow them to have confidence in you to work with their unconscious minds. In part this is about ethics – it *is* possible to go straight for the unconscious by using language directed at the unconscious mind, but this should never be done without explicit agreement from the client. The client is not 'done to' in coaching and all approaches to working with them need open discussion as equal partners. There is also the issue of rapport to consider – the principles explored earlier involving matching, pacing and leading. Many executive coaching clients knowingly or unknowingly place a high value on their own intellectual prowess – which is not surprising, given that this is where they have received, earlier in their careers, a primary sense of success and reward. Nor is it surprising given how society has historically honoured and rewarded intellectual achievement – 'clever' people tend to be looked up to and respected. So, in order for the coach to create and maintain rapport it is sometimes necessary to go along with this – in effect to match at the intellectual level until such time as the client can be safely 'paced' and 'led' to work with a sense of confidence in the unconscious realms. There is little point jumping the gun and introducing what are powerful techniques for reprogramming the unconscious mind if the client is intellectually resistant, and in any case for the reasons outlined above it would be disrespectful and unethical to attempt to do so.

Nonetheless, successful and powerful executives are no less prone to confidence issues than anyone else. A surprising number in fact report feelings of not being 'up to' their jobs, feeling that at some point they will be 'found out' – I have heard this referred to as 'impostor syndrome'.

Here are some typical confidence issues I meet in coaching senior executives:

- confidence in decision-making at a strategic level, e.g. 'Do we as an organization try to position ourselves as a large organization offering generic services or as a smaller one offering specialist services?'
- decision-making at personal levels, such as 'Do I go for this new job that will mean my moving into a new field in which I am no longer "king" but seen as an expert consultant?'
- presentation issues, such as speaking in public or being interviewed
- dealing with conflict, for example standing up for what you see as your rights at work or dealing with aggression
- dealing confidently with emotionally charged occasions, such as leaving a place of work after many years when you hate goodbyes
- needing to convince other 'important' people that your case or your proposal is the one they should adopt
- managing or chairing crucial meetings.

So what is confidence? It is an abstract state in some ways – we know when we 'have' it or do not 'have' it but it can be troublesome to define in absolute terms. In essence the word 'confidence' itself is a nominalization, that is, a category that is essentially meaningless without behavioural context: you can't 'have' confidence in a definitive way, you can only 'do' confidence, rather like you don't 'have' a relationship with someone in concrete terms, you relate *to* them in specific behavioural ways. So confidence is something we *do* rather than something we *have*. As such, confidence has structures and syntax within our behavioural and sensory experience and therefore can be learned and habituated to – confidence can be a habit.

It is definitely a 'whole person' phenomenon. To be confident we need to experience a range of states: physical, intellectual, emotional, even spiritual. Paul McKenna, in admirably ambitious language, refers to confidence as 'a level of comfort with yourself that can withstand the slings and arrows of outrageous fortune and carry you forward to the life of your dreams', and 'an attitude and approach to life that leads to success, motivation and new possibilities!'

When I think about circumstances in which I *personally* feel confident it seems to me that these states vary considerably in terms of the *context* in which confidence is needed. If I am feeling confident playing golf, for example, there is a particular combination of physical *control* combined with *relaxation*, a somehow 'optimal' state of mental alertness consisting of *clarity* of thought combined with a degree of *emptiness* of mind, a focus on perhaps two or three verbal instructions to the physical self. In addition, there are specific focuses and emphases of sensory perception. When playing golf, I know I am at my most confident when my internal *voice* is slow, soft and deep, my *visual* focus becomes sharply focused on individual objects (and ultimately before the shot, on the ball itself), and I *feel* a sense of unhurried, poised relaxation. Emotionally there is optimism combined with caution, excitement combined with calm, and an underlying sense of full commitment to each and every shot. This kind of state, regardless of context, is sometimes labelled as 'optimum arousal'.

When feeling confident during a coaching session, there is a subtly different syntax and grammar for each of these components, with different emphases and sequences. At the higher levels of beliefs and values there is a need to perceive that I am doing the right thing at the right time in the right place and for the right reasons. At the highest levels of 'being', confidence emerges from knowledge of appropriate connection and alignment. Sometimes it is hard to separate confidence from a range of other phenomena and states of being. Sometimes, too, confidence is a component of even higher states, and might be referred to as being in 'flow' or at 'peak experience' (see the account of the peak experience exercise on pp.111–13), or even 'a state of grace'. Academic studies sometimes seem to skirt round the subject. For example, in the fascinating book *Optimal Experience* by Mihaly and Isabella Selega Csikszentmihalyi, a psychological study of 'flow' in consciousness, the term 'confidence' is not even listed in the appendix: I could not find it in the indexes of numerous books on NLP and coaching, either.

So confidence is apparently ephemeral but, seemingly, essential. In essence, it is an active sequence of dynamic energies and accessible states that have been labelled, or nominalized, as something you can 'have' or 'be'. The trick is to be able to access it when you need it, to activate the appropriate sequences of sensory experience and active behaviours that work well. Often, too, when you examine the state we call confidence it turns out to be a whole lot of other things bundled together, such as boldness, familiarity or ease. Nonetheless, it comes up so frequently in coaching that it needs to be thought of as an important subject in itself.

As a coach, you can help your clients with their confidence issues using NLP-derived tools and techniques in numerous ways. This is one of the areas where NLP cannot lay unique claim to all of the helpful kit – it can hardly, for example, claim to have invented some of the breathing and muscular relaxation techniques, some of them thousands of years old, which can form a physical foundation for confident behaviour. But NLP is in essence the search for 'what works', and coaching is the drive to help someone tap into and utilize their resources, so it is all rock'n'roll – there is little to be gained for the coach by getting into some of the sniffy debates about who invented what or who has copyrighted what.

Confidence and strategic decision-making

Lucy was chief executive of an NHS mental health trust. A recent national reorganization had forced her to question the future shape and function of her organization. Ultimately, she would have to make a decision about what role, shape and function she wanted for her organization in the light of the proposed reorganizations, in order that she could begin to assemble her case for influencing government officials. In our coaching discussions, we mapped out the various options, considering the pros and cons of different models. As we went through this process, Lucy began to get increasingly edgy and to lose energy. I gave her some feedback on this and she said she was losing confidence in her ability to make a good decision because of the complexity and importance of the issues. This loss of confidence was leading to other issues for her such as anxiety and a loss of concentration. After some discussion, she agreed to try the technique of 'anchoring', and she was able as a result to tackle her decision in her usual forthright bold and confident manner.

Anchoring

In essence, anchoring is a way of gaining access to, and being able to hold on to, the states we need in order to be successful in a given context. It works on the same principle that is in place when a sensory stimulus puts us in mind of a particular time or context from our past. Essentially, anchoring is using a stimulus such as a sound, image, feeling, smell or taste that gives us a consistent response emotionally and even physically.

As I write this, I have just returned from walking my dog in the early evening late September sunshine in the New Forest. While there, the combination of rich reds and purples in the heather and bracken with the late summer sun, and a hint of chill in the breeze, brought back to me many occasions in the past, specifically long days in the Lake District hills and, even further back, the frisson of mixed excitement and resignation associated with the anticipation of a new year at school. The sensory stimulus of the particular combinations of colour and temperature reliably evoke these feelings and associations, thus 'anchoring' my state in the present to a state drawn from the past. You might like to think about some of the anchors you already have. Ones that work positively *for* you might include the following:

- a favourite piece of music (maybe 'our song')
- a particular scent or smell
- a sensation of touch – perhaps a particular fabric.

Negative anchors

You will also almost certainly have anchors that *don't* work for you, or work negatively – that 'Monday morning feeling' for example, or a particular location associated with a traumatic or unpleasant event. Maybe just seeing someone in the flesh will remind you of previous meetings that carry unpleasant memories. Remember, however, that we do have choices as to how we respond to the associations that crowd our lives. In building our life 'maps' we frequently create habitual responses to certain stimuli or situations that have a negative effect on us. You might think now about the sensations or situations that negatively affect your mood, attitude, motivation – and confidence. What are they? One of mine has been a dislike of cold, brightly lit interior spaces – they sometimes evoke rather painful feelings of abandonment and loneliness left over from childhood, and perhaps too much time spent in hospitals. I have sometimes experienced the effects of this 'anchoring' in places such as old-fashioned sports pavilions, connecting corridors in hospitals and other institutional settings. Numerous clients have described negative anchors – for example, feelings of dread associated with having to make presentations in particular settings, where the setting itself adds to the dread.

A useful way of lessening the habitual hold of these negative anchors is to develop the habit of self-awareness and awareness of the present moment – of being 'in the now'. This is a useful habit for numerous reasons, but specifically in this context it can give you the opportunity to feel far more in command of any negative feelings or states you may find yourself in as a result of being negatively anchored.

Positive anchors

Anchoring in NLP is the systematic process of dipping into the past to identify a resource state we were *once* in that would be useful to access and maintain in the present or future. The assumption or presupposition for the NLP coach to keep in mind here is that the client has all the resources they need – the client is essentially a resourceful person even when they are not currently in command of, or able to access, a resource they need. Anchoring is a tool the coach can use to help the client tap right back into the temporarily missing resource.

I have an anchor 'installed' in 1988 that still works for me very well: it is an anchor for calmness and boldness when I am in situations where my sometime fear of heights is a problem. The anchor is to press the fingers and thumbs of both hands together: this is discreet enough to get me through situations like getting into high external glass lifts without attracting any fuss. This anchor has been a good friend to me for all these years, allowing me to 'feel the fear and do it anyway'.

How to set a confidence anchor for your client

I always explain the whole process in outline to the client first in order to give them clear signposting about what it involves, how long it might take and so forth. This allows them to concentrate on the process itself when it is happening, without being distracted by thoughts about where it is going, or how much longer it will take.

I also emphasize to the client that I am going to need to know absolutely nothing of the *content* of what they are going to be anchoring – the process is all I will be involved in. This means they can be assured that the content remains absolutely private to them, with no need to interpret or explain to me as coach.

I also ask them in advance to select their choice of physical 'anchor'. This means a small physical action such as pressing forefinger and thumb together such as I describe above, or something else equally discreet like squeezing a wrist. It is important to get this detail right: the client needs an anchor that is sufficiently distinct not to get caught up in everyday behaviour but subtle enough for them to be able to use it when necessary in public without attracting attention. I explain that for the anchor to be most effectively created it will be important for them to notice when the feelings of confidence evoked are reaching their height, and to 'fire' their anchor (e.g. do the pressing together of fingers or squeezing of the wrist) when the feelings are on the rise, letting it go when the feelings begin to wane.

- Ask the client to relax. (This is most effective if you simply say something like 'Just relax for a few moments' rather than saying '*Try* to relax for a few moments' – their mind will listen to the word 'try' and it will become an effort.) Many clients instinctively close their eyes at this point. I sometimes suggest this to them in fact, by saying something like 'Many people find it useful to close their eyes.'
- Ask your client to think of a time in their past when they were at their most confident – it can be any time they remember clearly, from their recent past or even their distant past. Occasionally, clients demur a little at this point, saying things like 'Well, I never really *have* felt confident – that's why I need your help.' A little gentle enquiry or even challenge here can be appropriate – it may be, for example, that they have ignored moments in their lives when they have just taken confidence for granted without really noticing it. I have once or twice asked people if they feel confident when eating or reading, for example. You could even try asking if they are *sure* they have never been confident – sometimes the answer to this is an extremely confident-sounding (but highly ironic) 'No'. They do not necessarily need to have experienced 'conquering army' levels of confidence – just times when a *lack* of confidence has not been an issue may be sufficient to work with.
- Ask them to 'step into' this time when they felt at their most confident and see what was going on as if from their own eyes. Some clients need a little prompting to get this right, and I have sometimes found it useful to offer the metaphor of a film in which their eyes are the camera. This in NLP terminology is referred to as an 'associated' state, when they are 'in' the experience as opposed to a 'dissociated' state when they are looking at themselves from a distance. Associated states are more powerfully experienced and help to create a more potent anchor.
- Help the client to get into an intensely associated state by asking them to pay attention to the sights and sounds in their experience. It is important to use the present tense in order to keep the experience associated. I use expressions like 'Notice fully what you are seeing' or 'Be fully aware of the sounds you are hearing.' Sometimes, if the film metaphor seems to catch on for the client, I will ask them to imagine they are able to personally direct their film, creating exactly the kind of quality of sound and vision that they most enjoy.

- Ask them to notice their feeling of confidence as they continue to enjoy what they are seeing and hearing. Invite them to intensify the feeling and 'fire the anchor' (i.e. make the previously selected physical action) as the feelings approach their height.
- Gently invite them to 'step out' of their experience. Clients invariably enjoy what you have taken them through – after all, you are helping them to re-experience vividly a highly positive state of being.
- You may want to ask them to through the process again for themselves – once the sequence has been clearly established it only takes a matter of seconds, and repetition can strengthen the anchor.
- Ask the client to test the anchor in a future experience. Get them to imagine that they are in a future situation where they will need confidence, and as they imagine themselves in this future context ask them to activate the anchor. If the anchor has 'caught', they will be able to imagine themselves behaving with confidence in the future situation.

Lucy was able to take the technique on board with ease. I took her through the process with no idea whatsoever about the actual content of her associated experience. Lucy reverted back to the state she had been in before the temporary loss of confidence and we were able to help her get back on track with her strategic decision-making. Furthermore she had a tool she would be able to use in the future when seeking to influence others regarding the direction she wanted her organization to take.

Anchoring can be used to gather many other resources. These include courage, calmness and even compassion for self or others. Anchoring is a classic example of when the coach works entirely with the process, leaving all the content issues to the client. While you take the client through their 'film-editing' process you can have no idea of what they are working with – allowing them, among other things, the dignity of privacy.

Diana and the 'three demons' of performance

Confidence, or its lack, can manifest itself at many levels: physical, behavioural, emotional or intellectual. One of the simplest ways in which to begin the process of creating confidence is to deal with some of the physical aspects. Sometimes when people are called upon to 'perform', their thinking selves can get hijacked by their physical selves. Fortunately it is relatively easy to do something about these hijackings, but the trick is to be aware enough to take control of the situation before the situation takes control of you – or your client.

The three demons of performance are:

- shallow or inadequate breathing
- excessive muscular tension
- negative internal voice.

Diana was a client I saw many years ago, whose career was in jeopardy because her professional behaviour was to a degree out of control. She was a highly successful media editor whose extreme levels of passion for her programmes led to stress – she really could not bear the thought that her programmes could be anything other than perfect. This perfectionism had its 'up' sides of course, in terms of ensuring her constant drive to improve quality and creativity. But the serious downside was the anxiety – arguably the flipside of confidence – created by the felt need to control everything and everyone related to the production of the programme. The anxiety produced stress; the stress produced black moods and frequent angry outbursts towards her staff. As a result there had been a number of complaints made about her and there was a very real threat of her being removed from her post.

Much of our coaching was engaged with her coming to terms with the reality of her situation before she could even begin to think about doing something about it. The term 'denial' is one I am wary of using in a coaching context because of its psychotherapeutic connotations but it is probably appropriate here. Initially, Diana just could not see that anything was more important than the programme, and felt that virtually any behaviour on her part could and should be excused as long as the programme continued to be excellent. We had to work through this 'I am being treated so unfairly' agenda before Diana could recognize that confidence was at the heart of the issue. This in itself was significant learning for Diana. She had a mental picture of herself as a strong, achieving person and initially it was uncomfortable for her to recognize that there was a confidence dimension to her negative behaviour.

My initial coaching approach was to invite Diana to look in detail at the sequence of events that would occur in her thinking, her emotional state and her physical state prior to an angry outburst. Broadly speaking, the sequence would go something like this:

- She would experience intellectual dissatisfaction, for example about a graphic that in her estimation was not strong enough.
- This dissatisfaction would produce an emotional frustration and fear of producing something below standard.
- The fear and frustration would create anxiety about the viability and reputation of the programme, with which she was, in her mind, inextricably identified.

- This would create a crashing fall in her confidence state, causing panic, anger and thus outbursts of angry behaviour.

In short, anything that in her view would reflect badly on the image of the programme became translated very quickly in her mind into a direct threat to herself – to her identity. The perceived attack would almost simultaneously manifest itself physically as shallow breathing, muscle tension and a panicky, shrill internal voice predicting disaster.

This sequence would progress unnoticed by her conscious mind, which was fixed firmly on the issue of the script or the picture quality and her perceptions of inadequacy of those staff responsible. Ultimately she would lose control and blow up, shouting at and threatening her staff. When the storm had blown over she would be calm and confident once more, oblivious to the emotional storm-damage left behind and concerned only that the programme was back on a proper course.

The crux was that Diana was not aware of all the changes happening inside her until it was too late. We agreed that two steps were needed to give her the opportunity to maintain her state of confident wellbeing:

1. Develop a habit of 'checking in' with herself at regular intervals, i.e. to regularly pay attention to such things as her breathing, level of muscle tension and internal voice.
2. On the basis of the check-in, to make whatever adjustments seemed necessary.

Diana decided to wear a thread bracelet as an 'anchor' for confidence, and as a physical reminder to do the check-in: we agreed initially she would do this every fifteen minutes, and gradually she felt confident enough to lengthen the intervals between the check-ins. She is still in post and her output is as strong as ever.

Internal voice

Many of us talk to ourselves, though, thankfully, not out loud on the whole. So habitual is this self-talk for many of us that we can fail to pay conscious attention to it. Yet the messages from this internal voice often have a huge bearing on our abilities to deal with situations in the present moment. I first discovered this while working with clients on outdoor-based leadership programmes. From time to time we would engage in activities such as rock-climbing or high ropes courses. Client safety was of course absolutely guaranteed on these activities, but nonetheless from time to time someone would panic as the *perception* of danger, caused by exposure to height, overtook them. I could truly empathize with these clients as I sometimes struggled to control my own fear of heights, as described earlier. Imagine, then, someone gripping a rock-face some twenty or thirty feet above the ground, unable to move up or down, effectively frozen with fear. My job would be to coach them down, and a typical dialogue might go like this:

ME: Can you hear me? (I had learned that clients were sometimes so deafened by their internal voice that they were oblivious to the outside world.)

CLIENT: (in strangulated voice): Yes...

ME: Are you breathing?

CLIENT: (in even more strangulated voice): No...

ME: So *breathe* ... take some really deep breaths. OK ... how tense are your muscles right now?

CLIENT: (slightly less strangulated): Very ... I think I'm going to slip.

ME: Just be aware you can't fall – if you slip we'll hold you on the rope. You're completely safe, OK? OK?

CLIENT: OK.

ME: So just let your weight settle on your feet and legs. When you are ready you can take one arm off and give it a shake. Then the other one. Good. Now, what are you saying to yourself inside your head?

CLIENT: I'm going to fall – I might die!

ME: OK, so say to yourself *now* 'I am completely safe and I will be back on the ground in a few minutes.'

CLIENT: OK.

ME: OK, so keep breathing, stay relaxed and keep telling yourself you will be able to get yourself down safely. Now, listen to me...

At this point I would be able to give the client tips and direct instructions as to where to put their hands and feet in order to make their way down. This would not have been possible had the client still been listening to their negative inner voice.

The inner voice acts as a direct command. If you say to yourself you cannot do something, it is virtually guaranteed that you will indeed be incapable. If you say to yourself you *can* do something, you put yourself in a state where success is possible (though, sadly, not absolutely guaranteed). Paying attention to the internal voice puts you in a position to assert some control over the rest of your state. For example, I have worked with many clients who wanted to improve their presentation skills. Often, the critical positive difference in their confidence has been the moment when they realize they have a choice whether to listen to the internal voice saying something like 'They will all hate me, and I will dry up' or, instead, deliberately to choose to say something more positive as a message to themselves, like 'I really know my stuff and they will want me to do well.'

Sven-Göran Eriksson, the former England football coach, describes how he teaches this technique to his players for use when they have a particularly difficult, anxiety-provoking fixture. His approach is to give his players a kind of litany to repeat to themselves just prior to the game, something like 'I *can* do this, I *want* to do this, and I'm going to give it my very best shot.'

Thus, *awareness* of internal voice, levels of muscle tension and breathing (the 'three demons' of performance), followed by direct rectifying action, can be the express-speed key to unlocking and releasing natural physical and mental confidence. The apparent simplicity of this approach does not prevent it from being able to correct negatives in these three areas very quickly and effectively: with practice a wholesale change of state might take only ten seconds or so.

Peter and the need to be spontaneous: the 'nudge on the tiller' approach

Peter was a chief executive with a particular leadership challenge: he wanted to convey confidence to those around him and be more inspirational. He was already regarded as a highly competent and reliable manager, but through coaching realized that his real ambition was to raise his performance as a *leader* to the point where his personal example would create drive, confidence and even daring in others. He wanted to bring spontaneous flair to his leadership to add to his impeccable organizational and strategic thinking skills. Yet Peter was in appearance and behaviour as conservative and measured a figure as it was possible to imagine. He lived an extremely ordered life both at work and in the home, following a very strict timetable and pattern in both arenas.

As part of the coaching we explored what this unusual degree of orderliness was doing for him, and it transpired that he had developed these habits as a way of reasserting control over his life after a life-threatening illness. However, Peter recognized that for him to reach the next level of leadership skill he had to shed behaviours that could at times make him *appear* anxious, neurotic and over-controlled to his managers and staff. We began to discuss ways in which he could 'loosen the ties'. This was a metaphor that arose out of our discussion – it emerged as we were talking about his pristine dress sense. Our conversation helped Peter to recognize that his manner of dress was part of an overall pattern of over-control. One of the things that emerged, albeit as a light-hearted theme, was whether Peter would be prepared, during the hours of work, literally to loosen his tie. Peter initially arrived dressed with immaculate formality, and initially I dressed to match him; but as the theme of 'loosening up' developed I began to arrive for the sessions dressed more and more *informally* – deliberately aiming to send a message that a degree of informality did not equate to chaos. One day it happened – Peter undid his tie and loosened the knot perhaps three-quarters of an inch. We both laughed, knowing it was a significant moment, and Peter himself eventually saw it as symbolic of his readiness to make a change.

However, Peter made it clear that he felt very cautious about relaxing to any marked degree at work until he was convinced it would be somehow 'safe' to do so. Our earlier discussions had established that he felt personally as well as professionally secure within the boundaries of a very ordered regime. We began to explore how he might experiment with more safety at home, but as every avenue of possibility opened, Peter tended to close it down again. Eventually I challenged his commitment to change, and Peter finally agreed to a radical experiment. He would have his evening glass of wine at 9pm rather than 10pm as he (and his wife) had done for decades.

Peter reported back that this change had achieved two definite results – first, a realization that he really did not need such a strangulating schedule in order to survive and avoid loss of control, and second, a much happier wife. Peter went on to loosen up a lot at home, to the gratification of his family, and we finished our allotted sessions with a plan for him to extend his behaviour to his working practices.

The key point of Peter's story is that people often need to make change by small increments: confidence is developed by the creation of little victories – a succession of small but indisputable examples of positive behaviour change leading to the habits of confidence. As Aristotle said, 'We are what we repeatedly do. Excellence then is not an act, but a habit.'

A useful analogy is that of the giant oil super-tanker, long cited as an example of inertia in organizational change management seminars. 'Trying to change this organization is like trying to turn round an oil-tanker at sea' is the oft-heard cry. But oil tankers *do* of course turn round at sea, despite their huge momentum and inertia. The trick is not to try to turn them by main force, but to apply energy to a small section of the rudder that can in turn move the whole rudder, which in turn moves the ship around in the desired direction. The coach can help the client define the degree of turn that is tolerable to them and that does not require an overwhelming effort. This 'nudge on the tiller' approach has helped numerous clients who want to feel their way cautiously to change: who are not necessarily in any real crisis but who recognize that things could be better and more satisfying. By trying out new behaviours in small doses they create in their own mind the conditions for gradual but sustainable change.

Another example of this principle in action was Paul, a clever academic who labelled himself and his life as 'chaotic'. He had achieved a good level of personal success but was somewhat weighed down by the effort entailed by his lack of personal organization. In some ways his presentation of self and the picture he described of his life was consistent with popular views of the 'eccentric professor' – an office full of piles of paper, somewhat unkempt personal appearance and huge disorganization on both the personal and professional fronts. His 'nudge on the tiller' was to go away and tidy up a chest of drawers. Subsequent sessions identified further small but significant changes to his level of organization, until he reached a threshold of belief in himself as someone who could confidently manage himself as opposed to someone who felt scared and out of control.

Positive visualization: opening the batting for Australia

Try this simple experiment. Take a small personal behaviour you might like to change, for example being too physically tense in your shoulders and neck. Mentally rehearse a change in two different ways:

1. Concentrate hard on being less tense – try as hard as you can to relax.
2. Imagine yourself feeling soothed and relaxed, as a deep sense of ease effortlessly flows into you.

Which phraseology is more effective in producing relaxation? I remember at antenatal classes dutifully joining in the relaxation exercises along with the mums-to-be and other rather awkward-feeling dads. The nurse in charge would get us to lie down on the floor and then instruct us, in a voice that could strip wallpaper, to 'Try to relax!' The effect was to send shock-waves of tension into my system.

Visualization and mental rehearsal techniques are by no means unique to NLP, but NLP can work to a level of precision in the language that can produce particularly powerful results. NLP has drawn out many practical benefits from linguistic theory that create a direct impact on resourcefulness. A very simple example is the way in which NLP has taught emphasis on visualizing what someone really *wants* as opposed to visualizing what they *don't* want.

Some years ago on TV there was an interview with an Australian opening batsman who spoke frankly about his catastrophic decline in form and subsequent recovery. He explained how he had lost confidence in his technique in facing certain types of bowling. In an effort to overcome this he had embarked on a regime of mental rehearsal techniques. Unfortunately his form got even worse and he found himself repeating the same erroneous shots more and more frequently. Eventually he realized he had been mentally rehearsing *trying not to play the erroneous shots*. In so doing he had caused his mind inadvertently to rehearse the very shots he did *not* want to play, in order to imagine *not* playing them. As Paul McKenna says, 'Most people have spent their lives practising *stopping* themselves from going for what they want and then beating themselves up about doing such a good job of it.'

When using visualization techniques in NLP coaching, the aim is always mentally to rehearse successful outcomes using *positive* mental rehearsal. Thus, when a client comes to me seeking help with, for example, anxieties about a forthcoming important speech they have to make, or a critical meeting they have to chair, one approach open to me is to help them create a mental rehearsal in which they would imagine themselves succeeding, as opposed to imagining trying not to fail. I simply ask them to imagine themselves in the act of speaking at their very best, with all the associated feelings of confidence in place. I ask them to notice specific things about just what they are visualizing – what their posture is like, what their facial expression is like, how they are standing, and so forth. I also ask them to imagine what their voice sounds like, and even what their *internal* voice would be saying in their imagined confident state. If necessary we might add a confidence 'anchor'.

Confidence and the coach

Confidence is one of the key resource states that clients often feel they lack when facing challenging situations. However, it is not the only resource state that can go temporarily missing. The key for the coach is to hold on to their own belief that the needed resource state can be found. This can be challenging for the coach when a client presents as, for example, nervous or afraid. For inexperienced coaches there is sometimes a danger of getting infected by the client's current negative mood or behaviour – in effect, letting the client lead you and *your* resourcefulness downhill. It is useful at times like this to remember that you are working in partnership with the client – it is not your sole responsibility to solve all their issues.

Both NLP in particular and coaching in general hold as a primary principle that the client is a resourceful person, and one of the most effective ways coaches can help to bring this about is by modelling confidence in their *own* being. This might mean your learning to anchor your *own* resource states in order to be able positively to influence the client. Language is another key part of this, and it is essential to use language that assumes success for the client. As a coach you should avoid using language that in some way colludes with the client's fears and 'stuckness'. So, instead of saying something like 'Gosh, that does sound worrying – let's try to find a way forward' (implying that it will be difficult and hard work), say 'I can see this has been worrying you in the past, so let's look at the next steps forward to when you are going to be successful' (implying that success is assumed and the road to it has already begun).

You will find you can benefit from being coached yourself in how to be resourceful for your clients. Coaches are not superhuman and we need coaching too. Supervision of your coaching is a must.

I have also found it useful to use some of the NLP coaching techniques on myself. Specifically, I have found a self-applied meta-mirror (see Chapter 4) extremely useful when anticipating a particularly challenging client. Having practised the meta-mirror so many times, I now find it easy to do it quickly just in my head. I collect my feelings about the client, imagine being the client looking at me and how *they* might be feeling, take a detached view to allow myself the opportunity to create an outcome focus, and then quickly run through the fourth position script just to get myself 'resourced up' for the session. A simple variation on this is to imagine that there is a somewhat more confident 'you' sitting or standing some distance away from you. This 'you' might look a little different, perhaps with confidence expressed through a different look in the eyes or set of the shoulders. You can practise 'stepping into' the more confident you and experiencing how the world looks and feels. Repeat with ever more confident versions of yourself as required.

Sometimes I add a physical dimension to gathering confidence; in this case all I do is centre my body, lowering the weight that can sometimes shift upwards along with shoulder tension. I also pay attention to the internal voice, ensuring that it sounds slow, calm and deep. The effect is to make me feel more balanced, focused and calm. In cases of real nerves, thankfully few and far between these days, I might give myself a positive mental command along the lines of 'I can do this, and I want to do this, and it will go well.'

6 Helping the client get the most from their life and career

Some years ago our company, Management Futures Ltd, was holding an open day in London. Among the events of the day, we wanted to showcase our coaching approach. As a part of this I offered to coach anyone in the audience for twenty minutes on the promise of a free and confidential two-hour session to follow as reward. Up stepped a volunteer, a distinguished-looking man. I asked him what he would like to be coached on, carefully emphasizing that we were in front of a large group and only had twenty minutes at our disposal.

'Well,' he said, 'I'm 61 and I don't know what to do with the rest of my life.' I blinked a bit and asked him what he did for a living.

'I'm a professor of strategic management at X university,' he replied.

'I wonder if there are any resources you use in your job that you might apply in thinking about this issue?' I asked.

'Aha . . .' he said, as the light bulb came on. We went on to look at what tools of strategic thinking might help him specifically to think about his life.

This was a beautiful example of the coaching belief that the client is a resourceful person combined with the NLP presupposition that people have all the resources necessary to make any desired change.

Although the circumstances above could be described as dramatic, the issue itself was not unusual. We have coached hundreds of senior managers with issues such as the following:

- reaching a milestone birthday (often with a 5 or a 0 in it), or a career milestone, e.g. twenty-five years in the same organization, and experiencing this as a trigger for a career/life rethink
- facing a test of nerve or commitment, such as wanting to branch out into a new career or leave a job and start a new business
- concerns that their present job is not meeting their ideals or core values and is therefore offering them less fulfilment
- feeling that in some way they have not got what it takes to make the career progress they want, e.g. that they lack some skill, capability or personal quality
- simply not knowing what they want out of the rest of their career and therefore being unclear in focus

- wanting to rethink their career in the face of a change in their personal circumstances.

It is often the case that these issues involve complex combinations of factors, creating a degree of confusion and uncertainty for the client. There is very rarely in coaching a situation where a client comes in and states their issue and the coach smartly and straightforwardly deals with it with a single intervention or miracle technique. Magic bullets are few and far between in coaching. Therefore the techniques offered below will rarely be used in isolation or even in simple combination with each other, but form part of an overall coaching approach with a variety of techniques drawn from NLP and from various other sources. This is, to repeat, true of all the other descriptions of NLP techniques outlined in other chapters. The intention here is to offer tools you can use flexibly.

Benjamin was a client who decided to commit himself to an extensive programme of coaching in order to allow him to take stock and make progress in his work and life in general. Benjamin described his issues broadly as follows:

- dissatisfaction in current role as a specialist trainer in a local authority department – feeling confined and restricted by the specialist role and generally unsupported by his manager
- aspiration to set up his own training business focusing on management development
- a wish to make some important lifestyle changes, including buying a house near the coast.

Underlying these issues were deep fears. His father had always lived within tight financial constraints and Benjamin was deeply anxious about the prospects of an impoverished old age. Although only 40, he was tremendously concerned about the idea that he might weaken his pension entitlements and thus jeopardize future security. At the same time, he questioned his own ability to build a successful business. Benjamin was an intelligent man with broad and deep knowledge of the management development field. He also had many of the personal attributes that make a good management development trainer – he was articulate, emotionally intelligent and had presence, as well as a passion for the subject. In short, there seemed no convincing presenting reason that he should not achieve success in the business as a freelance trainer, one of his most important goals.

As we discussed his current work circumstances, he seemed miserably frustrated and unfulfilled in his current role. Not only that, he was financially frustrated, unable to afford to make the progress he wanted in the housing market. His business plan seemed credible and thorough, yet for many months he had been unable to bring himself to commit to leaving work and giving the business a go. Even when he managed to put in place a deal with his employers to guarantee enough income to meet his basic security needs on a part-time basis, he continued to prevaricate about taking the business plunge.

Benjamin's issues were complex. We worked together for several sessions, exploring his life and its lessons for him, unravelling the issues, clarifying his work and life goals, building a vision of success, strengthening his commitment to his professional and personal values. We also looked at potential sabotage factors, both external, in terms of business issues, and internal, in terms of doubts, worries and potential self-sabotaging behaviours and thought patterns. In short, we used a wide range of techniques both NLP and non-NLP derived on his issues, but there was to be no single breakthrough technique, no miracle solution.

This is sometimes the case in coaching – sometimes the patterns of thought, habits and beliefs that clients have built up over the decades of their lives are highly tenacious and operate 'underground', i.e. beneath the surface of the client's intellectual processing. It can take persistence and resourcefulness on the part of both coach and client to bear the frustration of making what can seem at times tortuously slow progress.

However, in this case progress we eventually made, and when we reviewed all of this work two techniques drawn from NLP seemed to have particular impact for Benjamin. One is concerned with spotting assumptions and presuppositions that contribute to self-limiting beliefs and the other with clarifying goals in a systematic and 'ecological' way, often referred to in NLP as well-formed outcomes.

Working with well-formed outcomes

As with most NLP techniques, if you read ten books you will get ten slightly different versions of the method. This is fine by me – in the end, NLP has to be owned by the user. I was first taught this process in 1988 and have modified it slightly since. Numerous clients and students have commented on how useful they found the criss-cross framework: first, because it gives them something visually memorable, and second, because it allows them to use the format flexibly and in sequence with their own thoughts, as opposed to following a list or some other rigid structure.

The essence of this simple model is that by using it, individuals get the opportunity to define a goal or outcome for themselves that stands a good chance of working because it has been very thoroughly thought through and tested. Consider the opposite phenomenon. It is New Year's Eve and you decide that *this* is going to be the year you lose weight/give up smoking/take up running/read all of Shakespeare, etc. How many of these resolutions last more than a few days? The key point here is that for clients in coaching to make real progress they need more than just a wish list or 'fool's goals' (pardon the pun). Indeed, encouraging clients to define goals in anything other than a rigorously thought-through way can actually be doing them a disservice, as in following these poorly defined goals they risk disappointment, disillusionment and a consequent fall-off in motivation. Coaching sessions are invariably fuzzy and unfocused unless really clear outcomes and goals are established. It is also true that as the issues relating to these goals and outcomes are discussed in depth during coaching they can change: the coach needs to be ready to redefine outcomes as the client learns more during the coaching process. This clear focus is one of the things that distinguishes coaching from much psychotherapy and counselling where the emphasis is more on creating an exploratory process.

Let's look at a scenario where a client is trying to get clarity on an important goal. I find it particularly helpful to draw out the framework in Figure 6.1.

I then talk through the framework in general terms to build their familiarity with it, and then talk through their goal or outcome frame by frame. Other than beginning in the top left box, there is no set order in which the boxes need to be visited – a factor that makes for flexibility and ease of use.

Box 1 (top left) this is almost always the place to begin because it asks the client to define their goal in *positive* terms. This is not just about being gung-ho. It is far more compelling and powerful to define what you *do* want rather than what you *don't* want. For example, if your outcome is expressed as 'losing weight' then your mind will automatically focus on your weight, i.e. will reinforce the negative, the very thing you want to change. (If you would like an example of how the brain works like this, try saying to yourself 'I will *not* think of pink elephants' and see what happens.)

Take a moment to think about something you perceive as a problem at work. In using this exercise over the past eighteen years I have yet to encounter a single individual who cannot do this. We have no problems being problem-focused, it seems. Now ask yourself the following questions about this problem, and notice your response, not just intellectually, but in terms of your personal resourcefulness, e.g. how empowered or motivated you feel to deal successfully with the problem:

- Whose fault is it?
- Why haven't you solved it yet?
- What barriers are in the way?
- What limitations do you have as a person in solving this?
- What are the forces outside your control that are conspiring against you?

Figure 6.1

- What other problem is this problem causing?
- What are the negative knock-on effects?
- What is having this problem saying about you as a professional? As a person?

How did you respond? Disregard the content of your answers for a moment and focus on the feelings they evoked. If your response is to leap into action, energized, confident and motivated, my experience of working with clients with these questions suggests you are in a very small minority. These questions are in essence *problem focused:* and for many of us, much of the time, problem focus becomes failure focus.

Now think about the *very same issue*, and answer the following questions, again noticing the effect upon your energy, confidence and motivation:

- In respect of this issue, what do you most want?

- What will getting what you want do for you?
- What positive knock-on effects will there be?
- How will you know you have achieved what you want? What will the evidence be, especially in what you will be seeing, hearing and feeling, both inside and outside yourself?
- What resources do you have as a person that will help you get what you want? Think about how you have succeeded in the past.
- What will getting what you want say about you as a professional? As a person?
- What is the next simple step you can take in getting what you want?
- When will you take it?

Notice the difference in the responses you get within yourself – and how much more positive and empowering they are. Everyone responds slightly differently to these questions but it is my overwhelming experience that the outcome or success-focused questions are a launch pad for at least the possibility of taking some action, however small, towards the goal. (An interesting side-effect of asking the two different types of questions is that many people notice that the problem *changes* in sensory terms, sometimes in terms of size, shape or colour, at other times in terms of feelings or sounds, even smell and taste. This in itself changes people's response to the issue as they first conceived it.)

In defining your outcome as, for example, 'becoming slim and fit', you start to focus the mind on what you actually *do* want. An example from a business context might be an initial negatively expressed goal of 'Stop arguing with my colleague' to be reformulated positively as 'I want to have much more productive discussions with my colleague.'

To define an issue in terms of outcome rather than problem is to create the beginnings of conditions for success: however, as many optimists have found, this in itself is not sufficient, so we need to move on to each of the other boxes to create truly well-formulated outcomes.

Box 2 (top centre) is often the next box to go to because it invites you to define *clear evidence* for your goal's being achieved. In defining outcomes that do not have clear, quantifiable evidence this is particularly important because it crystallizes for the mind exactly what you are going for. Specifically, it is important to create sensory evidence for success: literally, how success will look, sound and feel – even how it will smell and taste! Otherwise, all the mind will have is a concept or idea without anything compelling to attract it. The more evidence for success you are able to describe, the more compelling it will be. A good example might be that of a manager I worked with who wanted her team to be 'more cohesive and positive'. I encouraged her to think about what she would actually be seeing, hearing and feeling that would enable her to *know* that that was how the team would be behaving. She described things like seeing the team spending more time discussing things together, and people being able to offer feedback and even criticism in an open way. These descriptions made it much easier for her to communicate what she really wanted to her team.

Box 3 (top right) is about the degree of *control* you have personally in achieving your outcome. There is little point in committing to outcomes over which you have little control – indeed this is a recipe for disappointment and reduced future motivation. Setting as an outcome becoming younger, taller and more handsome, for example, is doomed to failure – I know this for sure having tried for it many times. If your outcome involves other people in any way it is important to weigh up just how much you can personally be responsible for starting and maintaining progress towards it.

Box 4 (centre box) is about context for your outcome. Where and when and with whom do you want your outcome? Are you clear too about any potential knock-on effects for your outcome in other areas of your life – does it fit the overall *ecology* of your life in a healthy way? It is also important to know in what contexts your outcome is *not* wanted. For example, if a client decides they want to do much more delegation of work, it is important for them to check just where the limits of this are – including considering just how much delegation is really appropriate, and to whom, and of what nature.

Box 5 (centre left) brings into focus something very practical indeed – money. It is surprising how many outcomes involve some kind of financial dimension or implication, and this box invites you to consider this area carefully before committing to pursuing a particular outcome. It can be useful to cross-check with the centre box (context), for example asking how the financial implications of your proposed outcome might affect the various contexts of your life – is your outcome financially ecological?

Box 6 (bottom left) relates to time factors. It is more than a 'by when will this outcome be achieved?' box – it reminds you to consider how much time your outcome might take and whether this is ecological in the context of your overall goals. You may decide, for example, to learn a foreign language: all the other boxes seem to work through without any problems and then you check out the time box, only to realize that you would need to spend an hour a day to achieve your goal – just when you have started redecorating the house. You may decide to defer the language project for a couple of months until you can give it the time it needs.

Box 7 (bottom centre) invites you to consider the overall worthiness or worthwhileness of your goals. This might include, for example, the amount of effort it is worth putting into pursuing a particular outcome. Is it important enough in the context of everything else you are trying to achieve? Does it dovetail well with other outcomes? Is it really worthy of all the effort it might take?

Box 8 (bottom right) is a check on personal values. Does this outcome feel right? Is it consistent with who I am and who I want to be? Are there any conflicts in values created by the pursuit of this particular outcome? In short, does it reflect me as I want to be?

A great way for the coach to check out the level of congruence a client might have with their stated goal is to check out their *body language* as they consider this box, and indeed as they work through the framework in general. You might look out for signs of doubt or discomfort in the body language, and at the general energy level or level of enthusiasm the client is displaying. Should you have any doubts in this area you might usefully offer them to the client using the 'feedback in the here and now' technique – describing their behaviour and its impact on you. It is particularly important not to let your observations or impressions go unheeded by you or your client here, as the outcomes to which they are committing really need to feel right for them in all dimensions of their being if they are going to work for them.

Box 9 (centre right) is important and one of the most potent parts of the well-formed outcome process. It invites you to consider (a) what you might stand to *lose* if you are successful in your outcome, and (b) what you might get out of *not* achieving it. Most change incurs some kind of loss, no matter how desirable the change is. I can think of numerous examples of this from coaching where, let's say, someone achieves their goal of the big promotion only to find themselves over-challenged, overworked and in a very different set of relationships with their former peers, and find themselves miserable as a result. On the other side of the coin, it is often the case that what is stopping you making a change is the fact that you are getting a lot out of staying just as you are. For example, someone who says they want to argue less with their spouse may, on deeper examination, realize that the reason they argue is that they enjoy the drama and the attention they are getting. In these cases it can be important for the coach to discuss with the client how else they might get these important needs met in order that they can pursue progress towards their desired outcome. In any case, it is imperative that the downsides of getting what you want are fully weighed in the balance; otherwise, you may find yourself unconsciously sabotaging progress towards your goal.

Summary

As a coach you can use this method to help clients clarify goals that are really worth comitting to. You will be providing the process framework and the encouragement; the client will provide all the content – the thoughts, feelings, pictures and sounds that embody their goals.

As with most NLP, and indeed most coaching, the coach needs to know little or nothing about this content. An additional benefit of this is that the client is able to consider their personal content in private, with no pressure whatsoever to disclose the thoughts, feelings, pictures, sounds, etc. with which they are working. For example, when taking the client through box 2, the box that invites the client to consider the evidence they would look for to know their outcome had been achieved, all the coach really needs to do is make the suggestion that the client should see, hear and feel what they would want to be happening: there is no need for the client to 'report back' to the coach in detail. This dignity of privacy in itself is a hugely beneficial part of coaching, and especially coaching with NLP. All clients hold things back from their coach, for a variety of reasons, and pressure from the coach to disclose or reveal what may be sensitive content is likely to lead to defensiveness of one sort or another on the part of the client.

Physical dimensions of an outcome/success focus

Outcome focus is not just about the words the coach uses. The words are only part of the interactive mind/body/spirit combination that forms our being. Here is an exercise you can try for yourself.

Think of a current work problem: think of it, for the time being, deliberately as a *problem*, asking all the problem-focused questions outlined above – the ones beginning with 'Whose fault is it?' As you ask yourself these questions, allow your body to shift into a problem-framed state – perhaps you might sit in a slumped position, looking down to the floor. Notice as you ask and answer these questions how the problem *looks, sounds* and *feels* inside your head.

Next, go outside and start walking. As you walk, coach yourself into a state of really positive walking – as close to perfect as you can make it. Things to work with in this self-coaching might include attention to posture, rhythm, pace, keeping your head up, arm-swinging and so forth. The point is to walk in a way that *you* judge to be optimal for yourself.

When you think your walk cannot be improved upon, revisit the problem you thought of to begin with, *but maintain the positive walking state as you do so – this is important if the exercise is to work properly*. Notice how your perception of the problem changes in the way it represents itself to your senses – what you see, hear and feel. Most people notice very significant and positive changes in the way they are experiencing the original 'problem' while walking in this positive way – changes in the shape, size and colour of the problem, for example. A lot of people find it difficult to even see the 'problem' as a problem any more! At the very least there will be a change of some sort in the way the original issue is perceived. For those of you committed to a problem focus there is no need to worry – you still have the choice to see your issue in this way whenever you choose.

Once you have coached yourself through this exercise it is of course perfectly possible for you to coach a client through the same process. I have done this many times, either just to bring a different set of resources to a client or to help them to realize the degree to which their physical state has an influence on their thinking and their outlook on the issue they are working on. To summarize the steps:

- Get the client to focus on their 'problem' while in a 'negative' physical state, e.g. slumped, shallow breathing, eyes rooted to the floor. Get them to notice how they perceive the problem and how they feel when they do this.
- Take them outside and coach them in 'perfect' walking, that is, walking in the way that feels best for them. Coaching in this context means asking them to walk how they feel best, but may include a few prompts asking them to pay attention to things like breathing, rhythm and pace.
- When they are walking at their best (as judged by them), get them to mentally revisit the initial 'problem'.
- Discuss with them the differences in their perception of the issue when viewed from the two distinct physical states, and to compare their levels of resourcefulness.

The *whole* of your being, including the physical, is involved in the way you construct and interpret your experience. As a coach I try to be aware of how *my* physical state is impacting on the experience of the client. What would be the point, for example, of attempting to help a client access a resourceful state, let's say optimism, while in my physical being I am modelling boredom or lack of enthusiasm?

As a coach you can also encourage your client to think about the physical state they might want to be in if they are to feel fully resourceful in a particular way. A simple way of getting them into this is to ask them to imagine themselves at their most resourceful and notice what the physical aspects of 'most resourceful' are – what they see, hear and feel in themselves in the resourceful state of being. A simple exercise that might help here is to get them to imagine a version of themselves standing a few feet away that embodies a resourceful state – let's say, 'optimism'. Get them to notice how this 'optimistic' self looks, sounds and feels and have them 'step into' this version of themselves, imagining themselves moving into the more optimistic version.

Working with negative assumptions, presuppositions and self-limiting beliefs

Many people carry around with them a number of beliefs that have held them back for years. Typically, these beliefs are formed in early life, sometimes as the result of a single high-impact event or because of the behaviour of a significant adult such as parent or teacher. These early beliefs are powerful and can remain deeply embedded throughout adult life. Despite our intellectual maturation as adults, we can behave and act according to this early scripting.

Beliefs are not necessarily about the 'big' things such as ethical principles or ideology. At the personal level they are, in effect, the rules of your life – what you should/shouldn't, must/mustn't do. Sometimes these beliefs are highly empowering, giving you permission and structure to achieve your goals and live the way you want to. At other times, these rules are about limitation and obstruction, a constant rigid source of negative compulsion and expectation.

The logical levels model

Robert Dilts created the *logical levels* model in 1987. The model illustrates, among other things, how fundamental beliefs are in shaping our behaviour, core habits and character and, ultimately, aspects of our destiny (see Figure 6.2).

Beginning from the top, the model suggests suggests that we are all connected beings, and that our *connectedness* is at the core of our *spiritual* nature: we are all part of something bigger than we are. At the next level, we experience our *core identity*, that essence of unique mental energy by which we recognize ourselves. The next level concerns our *core beliefs* and the consequent *values* by which we shape our lives: this level is so very close to the identity level that sometimes people think that they *are* in effect their beliefs. This goes some way to explaining why people can be extremely reluctant to have their beliefs challenged in any way. If we want to see evidence of beliefs and values in action, we need look no further than the daily news in which we see people sacrificing their own lives or ending the lives of others in pursuit of their beliefs.

People often behave as if their beliefs were true, and value them in reality more than the teachings of the gurus and saints. At a seminar I attended a couple of years ago, the consultant and writer Adrian Gilpin asked us in the audience to identify in our minds some of the behaviours in others we found annoying. A number of people mentioned lateness/unpunctuality. Adrian asked one woman in the audience what she wanted to *do* to people who were

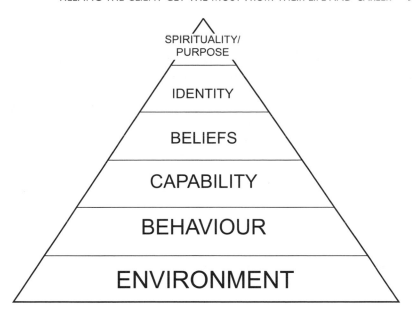

Figure 6.2

late or kept her waiting: her reply was something like 'Hit them! Slap them! *Kill* them!' Far from this being greeted with nervous astonishment at the presence of a homicidal maniac in our midst, many in the audience shouted their support for her sentiments, cheering her on wildly. Adrian, after calming the mob, went on to discuss how we would often rather be 'right', i.e. *to have our beliefs validated*, than exercise compassion or even, as he put it, our humanity. As a coach you need to recognize the power of the client's prevalent belief and value system and treat it with due respect. Clients will not thank you for criticizing their core beliefs and values, even if it is evident to you as coach that they are not serving the client particularly well in the present day.

At the next logical level, our beliefs and values affect our *capabilities* – our capacities and skills. Moving down to the next level, we have our actual *behaviours* – the specific actions in our lives. All of the five preceding levels take place in the context of our personal *environment* – the combination of things, factors and relationships that make up the individual fabric of the world in which we personally live. All the levels interact dynamically to create a mental map of ourselves.

Meta-patterns and the 'towards – away from' continuum

In NLP, 'meta-pattern' is the name given to the governing patterns of our lives, the 'big architecture' of our habitual thinking and ways of looking at the world. These meta-patterns can link usefully to the logical levels model. Sometimes they are described as ways in which we sort information, experience, thoughts and feelings into recognizable patterns. A useful way of thinking about these patterns is to think of polar opposite ways of looking at things, for example:

- future orientation ↔ past orientation
- focus on what is right ↔ focus on what is wrong
- focus on past ↔ focus on future
- assumption of plenty ↔ assumption of scarcity
- towards what is wanted ↔ away from what is not wanted
- can do ↔ can't do
- proactive ↔ reactive
- focus on similarity ↔ focus on difference.

From the bottom to the top of the logical levels pyramid, the following questions based on meta-patterns are useful in coaching someone around life and career issues:

1. *Environment* (e.g. home, workspace and travel)
   Typical question: 'At the environmental level, what are you seeking to move *away from* and what are you seeking to move *towards*?' This question usually involves the client in thinking about the balance of work and home, the amount of travel they want or don't want, whether they want to work in a team or alone and even things like the status of office to which they aspire.
2. *Behaviour* (e.g. kinds of work task and methods of working)
   Typical question: 'At the behavioural level, what are you seeking to move away from and what are you seeking to move towards?' This question allows clients to think in detail about the kind of activities they really want to be focusing on in future, e.g. moving *away* from operational management and *towards* more strategic thinking.
3. *Capabilities* (e.g. skills, use of talents)
   Typical questions: 'At the level of capability, what skills or talents are you hoping to develop and make more use of? What new skills would you hope to learn and use, and which might be passing their sell-by date?' These questions or similar ones enable the client to explore what they want to move towards in terms of their personal growth, learning and development.

4. *Values and beliefs* (e.g. the realms of significant meaning, purpose and structure)
   Typical questions: 'What core values are you moving towards in your life and career? Which are becoming less important? What beliefs about yourself are really important to move towards? And what old beliefs are you looking to leave behind?' These and similar questions are another way of encouraging clients to engage actively in looking at what is often implicit and even unconscious in their motivation. A benefit of looking at values and beliefs in this way is that it implies a sense of dynamic development, whereby values and beliefs are more than abstract nominal constructs but are seen as active, organizing components of a developing life.

5. *Identity* (who you are)
   Typical questions: 'What kind of person are you hoping to become? What do you see as your core, defining personal mission in life?' These are big, high-impact questions and need to be employed sensitively and with full rapport engaged if they are not to present as overwhelming or intrusive to some clients. However, they are also questions that create a great deal of thought and really focus a client on the crux of their being.

6. *Spirituality/purpose*
   Typical questions: 'How does your mission fit into the wider world? How does it connect with the bigger systems of which you are a part? What kind of connection are you moving towards?'

Incidentally, you do not have to make this into a 'technique' as such for the client. You can ask the questions as a part of a regular-sounding conversation – you being aware of the structure you are following, but leaving the client free to dwell on the meaning and the exploration.

Beliefs profoundly affect, and indeed create, specific capabilities and actual behaviours, and these capabilities and behaviours in turn affect beliefs in a reinforcing loop. I have had many discussions with clients about how their thinking or behaviour at one level impacts upon their thinking and behaviour at another. For example, I remember working with an executive who had made it to the top from very humble beginnings. He had been brought up in a tough district of Glasgow (environment) where he had learned that it was sometimes necessary to protect yourself with verbal and even physical aggression (behaviour). His beliefs about self-protection still had this Glasgow overlay, and as a result he would frequently lash out verbally in the context of both his work and his private life. While he recognized that this was not appropriate in his current life environment he still felt deep in his belief system that you had to be a tough guy to make it. Rather than attempt to change this belief wholesale, I discussed with him other models of 'toughness' that did not require aggression, and he was able to recognize that it was possible to be tough in a non-aggressive way. The final step was to get him to take action, and this involved him agreeing to notice in future when he was tempted to act aggressively and to act with reasonableness and control instead. Gradually he was able to build up confidence in a new belief that he could survive in the present day without resorting to aggression. Interestingly, this had the additional benefit of actually making him feel 'tougher' in himself because he enjoyed the feeling of greater self-control and self-management.

Sometimes our beliefs act as blueprints for our future – they are actually self-fulfilling prophecies. For example, if you live your life believing you can achieve anything you put your intention or will to, the likelihood is that you will achieve much of what you set out to do. Conversely, if you believe that most of what you attempt is likely to fail, you will not bring your full resources into play and failure is the likely result. As someone once said, 'If you believe you can, or if you believe you can't, you're right!'

Our beliefs therefore are emphatically not theoretical: they are evidenced in our every behaviour and word. I remember when I worked as an outdoor management trainer in the Lake District how much someone's belief patterns would affect their enjoyment of, and success in, taking on sometimes challenging activities. For example, there was a ropes course on site (not an obstacle course requiring brute strength and raw courage, but a carefully constructed series of challenges requiring thought and, at times, a degree of commitment). The primary purpose of the ropes course was to help develop expertise in support and communication among teams, but there were many times when the challenging parts involving height and perception of risk created moments of drama for individuals. These dramas were often illustrations of beliefs in action. I would often coach people struggling in the middle of the action on the ropes course and in so doing was struck by the almost 100 per cent of cases in which a negative belief expressed in their internal dialogue ('I can't do this' or 'I'm going to come to harm') would create an inability to succeed. Conversely, the majority of those whose assumption was that they could succeed would indeed succeed – but sadly, it seems this cannot be taken as an *absolute* guarantee. As a rule of thumb, it seemed that if you believed you could not succeed you were almost certainly not going to, whereas if you *believed* success was at least a possibility then you were in with a good chance.

Often our negative beliefs are highly significant, sometimes relating to our deepest fears about our ability to survive emotionally, socially or even physically. Because of the very power of these beliefs we can sometimes unconsciously sabotage ourselves, in terms of both managing our relationships and getting what we want out of life. Typical self-limiting beliefs in coaching include the following:

- I am not loveable.
- I am a failure in some way.
- I have no real power.
- Others are not to be trusted.
- Other people are to blame for my bad feelings.
- I/you/others can never really change.

In the context of work these beliefs are sometimes varied, extrapolated or transmuted into unhelpful patterns of beliefs such as the following:

- Fear of the gutter, e.g. make one mistake at work and I will be impoverished.
- It's all my fault – nothing or no one else can ever be to blame.
- It's not fair, e.g. other people get away with murder and never get the punishment they deserve and meanwhile I slog away and get no credit.
- My past defines me, e.g. I have become defined as a person by some terrible event in the past and this means that nothing can ever be right for me in the present or future.

We get so used to carrying these beliefs around that we take them to be true. In NLP, beliefs and the belief structures that we all have are not taken to be rigid and immovable. Instead they are seen as part of the totality of mind and are open to change – we have choices, even in our beliefs.

In practice, I have sometimes found clients in coaching profoundly resistant to even the *idea* that you/they can change even a tiny part of their beliefs – they believe that you cannot and *should not* change them. This is partly because beliefs are so hugely important to us – they give structure and meaning to our lives. People sometimes see their beliefs as things that 'belong' to them, as treasured possessions that give their identity extra grounding.

Therefore, when using belief-modifying techniques in coaching, one should aim for profound respect and reassurance as a foundation attitude. Beliefs form out of the unique personal history of the individual and are there for a reason. Helping someone to see the acquisition of a new, more empowering belief should not create a sense of loss in any way – only the offer of greater personal choice and freedom.

Working to change self-limiting beliefs is a matter of great sensitivity, but also has the potential to create really high-impact change for a client. NLP shows us how to do belief change work at a number of levels of complexity, from simply checking in with the congruence of a client's body language right through to quite structured belief-changing techniques.

Generalizations, deletions and distortions

Descriptions of generalizations, deletions, and distortions fall out of what in NLP is referred to as the 'meta-model', a set of ideas properly acclaimed as some of the most important of the NLP models, forming part of the foundation work of Richard Bandler and John Grinder. In essence, the meta-model is about how our language patterns not only represent an *expression* of our internal experience but also serve to *create* it.

At its most basic, the model teaches us some language patterns that may be creating or reinforcing erroneous or unhelpful assumptions about the world and our ability to function in it. Thankfully, the model also provides us with neat and simple ways of unpicking such assumptions, by asking questions beginning with 'what', 'how', 'who' or 'when'.

Generalizations, deletions and distortions are three of the most common self-limiting language patterns described in the meta-model. The trick in coaching is to look for missing bits of information and then to ask for them.

Dealing with generalizations

Many generalizations are useful. It is comforting and time-saving to know that, having eaten one apple and enjoyed it, the next apple is probably going to be good too. When you switch on the new TV for the first time it is indeed useful to assume that it will come on again next time if you press the same button. Learning to drive on a particular type of car teaches some principles and behaviours useful to transfer to how you might approach driving a slightly different type of car, and so on. These are the kinds of generalization that create helpful and time-saving habits. We learn a lot by generalizing, too, as in the rules of mathematics, science or grammar.

However, by no means all generalizations are so helpful. Sometimes we have powerful experiences in our lives that cause us to classify things in an unhelpful and potentially limiting way in our minds. Suppose, for example, that as a small child you lend someone a favourite toy and it is not returned: you may well respond by generalizing, consciously or unconsciously, with some kind of message to yourself along the lines of 'people cannot be trusted'. This message may persist, guiding your awareness and perception to notice only examples of the principle in action, deleting from your awareness examples of the opposite, i.e. trustworthy behaviour.

It is interesting to consider how this operates. Most of us in a 'common-sense' way probably assume that the phrase 'seeing is believing' accurately describes the process by which we take in information and data in a neutral way and then filter it through our belief system to create meaning. There is another school of thought that suggests a better principle might be that of 'believing is seeing': under this principle we *pre-filter* our sensory experience through our belief system, thus only seeing the kinds of behaviour we are pre-programmed to believe exist, and deleting any counter-examples.

In coaching, you will know a potentially unhelpful generalization is in force when your client makes an assertion including words like 'always' or 'never', e.g. 'You can *never* get anything to change around here', or 'I *always* get the blame for anything that goes wrong.' Listening out for repeated or emphatically expressed examples of these assertions creates an opportunity for the coach to provide constructive challenge. For example, if a client says something like 'I'm always getting blamed for everything in my office', the coach can reply with something like 'Everything? Always? What has happened ever that you didn't get blamed for?' For many clients this kind of simple and light challenge produces two simultaneous reactions: one is laughter, as they realize the literal inaccuracy of what they are saying, and the other is the beginnings of recognition that they may in fact have a habit of negative generalization that is creating a sense in them of, in this case, disempowerment or victimization.

Dealing with deletions

Deletions are essentially the parts of the client's mental model that seem to be missing as they describe something. The missing bits can be nouns or verbs or simple bits of information of various sorts. The effect of their omission is to create vagueness and non-specificity in what someone might be saying.

For example, a client may say something like 'She made me feel bad.' There are several missing bits here, including 'how' she did this and 'what' the bad feeling is or was. A useful coaching response might be to ask, 'How did she make you feel bad, specifically?' and then, later, 'In what way did she make you feel bad?'

Another pattern is for someone to delete a necessary comparison that gives context to an assertion. For example, 'My boss is awful' might invite from the coach the response: 'Awful in what way? Compared to whom?'

Sometimes clients turn what should be verbs or action words into nouns in a way that can create a sense of stuckness. For example, an assertion like 'Our relationship is really bad' creates an assumption that the relationship is a static entity. The coach can ask questions like 'What is going on that is bad, specifically?', thus searching both for specificity and for actual behaviours that can potentially be changed.

Dealing with distortions

There are several ways in which clients can inadvertently distort their view of an issue. One is to make a potentially erroneous assumption, for example 'She said that to me and that means she doesn't like me.' In this kind of example the coach can ask something like 'How does her saying that mean she doesn't like you, specifically?'

Another example is when clients 'mind-read' other people, for example saying something like 'I know you think I'm being silly' to their coach: here the coach can simply ask, 'What makes you think that I think that about you?'

There are numerous other examples in the meta-model of specific formulations of words that carry with them questionable assumptions or conclusions and views drawn from distorted, deleted or generalized information. For the coach the task is to ask, 'What piece of information is missing here that it might be useful for the client to focus on?'

Belief-busting

Sometimes, the relative simplicity of the meta-model challenges is not enough to shift a stubborn belief. In Benjamin's case there seemed to be an underpinning belief that *prosperity* was somehow not within his grasp, and that he would have to live his life according to the scarcity model exemplified by his parental upbringing. This belief was one of the major inhibitors to his goal of achieving business success. I clearly remember his emotional response to my proffering some information about the potential high earnings, relatively speaking, of freelance trainers in comparison with those working in-house: his facial expression, and subsequent words, was tantalizingly poised between wanting to believe me and *daring* himself to believe that what he had dreamed about could actually be within his grasp.

Thankfully Benjamin, as a highly intelligent client, was willing and able to grasp intellectually the concept of the self-limiting belief and was willing for his beliefs about scarcity and prosperity to be challenged in coaching. I discussed with him something of the theory of self-limiting beliefs and then asked him to focus on the following questions:

- What actually is the belief that limits you? Describe it in a sentence that begins 'I believe...'
- How was this belief created? Think of the time in your personal history when this belief was created, and identify the circumstances and the people involved.
- What has this belief done for you in the past? How has it tried to serve you (regardless of any unwanted negative consequences)?
- How is the belief now limiting you?
- What would you rather believe? Create a sentence beginning 'I would like to believe...'
- What behaviour(s), however apparently small, could you now take on that would be consistent with what you would prefer to believe?
- What will you actually commit to doing?
- How will you/we check your progress?

It is important in all coaching exercises to obey the rules of rapport and ask the questions using a style and form of words that enable you and the client to feel comfortable – it is counter-productive for the technique to get in the way of the client's process. Note also that it is the *commitment to try a new behaviour* that is at the business end of this technique – taking on a new behaviour, no matter how small, powerfully challenges old beliefs. Notice that the 'old' belief is still given explicit respect in the questioning process.

A colleague once explained this to me much more simply by saying, 'It is easier to behave your way into a new way of thinking than it is to think your way into a new way of behaving' – a useful thought to have if your coaching conversations are getting a bit bogged down in the theoretical or analytical.

For Benjamin, the issues of self-limiting beliefs were firmly attached to his needs for security. For me as a coach the challenge was to help him find a mindset that allowed him really to believe that the pursuit of prosperity and security simultaneously were not incompatible goals. This meant using the belief-busting questions to look into his assumptions around risk-taking and caution. We were gradually able to construct a convincing model that allowed Benjamin to take the 'risk' and start his own business – a dream that had been deferred for years out of caution, with a resulting sense of frustration and lack of fulfilment for him.

Specifically, we changed some ancient and rigid assumptions. For example, we examined his assumption that working for a local authority was somehow the 'safe' option. We concluded that all employees were vulnerable to organizational tides, i.e. you could get 100 per cent sacked whether you were any good at your job or not. If working for yourself, however, and you lose a client, it is unlikely to be the case that you lose all your income – if you have ten customers and lose a couple, you are only 20 per cent 'sacked' and you are still able to go out looking for more business. Furthermore, we discussed how talent and good work in your own business was likely to bring you work and consequent prosperity, whereas in a job there was, sadly, less likely to be a direct link between good work and prosperity, given the sometimes unfair way in which organizations can operate.

Colin

Colin, a finance manager who wanted to set up his own consulting practice, held the conviction that he did not have enough professional credibility to succeed in his own business, i.e. that he had cut off his options by working too long in the same organization in the same area of work. We gradually examined this self-limiting belief in the light of what Colin himself knew about people who had gone into the freelance market with success. Colin came to realize that he had more than enough knowledge and experience to match theirs. The critical realization, however, was his recognition that it was not past record on which business success depended – it was on performance in the here-and-now, working face to face with business clients in meetings and with actual people on courses. In training, you can only be successful *in the present* – even your last performance, however good, is not an indicator of success in the mind of the present customer in the moment you are dealing with them.

This realization was a huge release for Colin, who had been hung up on self-limiting beliefs about qualifications and track record for many years. He knew that his real strengths were in the area of relationship-building and in managing group dynamics and building learning environments – the very areas likely to bring success in business as a freelance trainer.

I am pleased to say that Colin made his transition successfully. Indeed, his level of success in his new business has brought with it some *new* issues, such as the need to manage his time effectively and allow him to enjoy himself and rest.

The ABCDE model

Mainstream psychology is increasingly in alignment with this kind of happiness-focused approach. The 'positive psychology' movement has begun to shift the polarity of psychological intervention away from trying to solve problems and towards trying to help people create more happiness in their lives. In essence the move is a parallel to NLP's emphasis away from 'problem focus' and towards 'outcome focus'. In his fascinating book *Authentic Happiness*, Martin Seligman (2003) outlines an alternative approach to belief-busting, based on a process of increasing optimism by disputing pessimistic thoughts. He calls this the ABCDE model. Once you recognise you have a pessimistic thought about yourself, you apply the model as follows:

- **A** stands for *adversity* – the recognition and naming of the circumstances that have initially created the pessimistic or self-limiting thought.
- **B** stands for *belief* – the belief issuing from the event and the thoughts/feelings created by it.
- **C** stands for *consequences* – the effects of the belief upon one's wellbeing.
- **D** stands for *disputation* – the core technique here is to dispute your own thought/belief as if you are an external person: Seligman points out that we are often good at disputing with others but rarely use the same skills to dispute negatives in our own lives.
- **E** stands for *energization* – the positive energy that follows a successful disputation.

I include this technique primarily as an illustration that NLP is not alone in developing practical techniques for helping people to deal positively with their issues, but as a coach you can adapt this technique to your own coaching style. Here is an example of how it works, drawn from working with Richard:

- *Adversity*: 'I came home late after a difficult journey and in a bad mood from work. My wife started to moan at me about her day and her feelings of being trapped in the house, and also complained about having to pick up after everybody, and how nobody seemed to thank her for everything she did for them. I snapped at her really hard, saying no-one was keeping her prisoner, and she could leave if she wanted, if she didn't like it here – way over-the-top stuff.'
- *Belief*: 'This marriage is going downhill fast. She doesn't appreciate all the work I have to do day in and day out – no one says thanks to *me* for my twelve-hour days and getting up at six every morning. She's bored with me – maybe I'm a disappointment to her . . .'
- *Consequences*: 'I sat and sulked while she stomped upstairs, but I knew I'd gone too far. After a while I got up and went upstairs. She'd clearly been crying. I said sorry, and she said it was OK, but she looked really shaken and hurt. I felt like a bully and a persecutor.'
- *Disputation*: 'This isn't the end of the world. We hardly ever have a spat, and when we do we always get round to discussing it sensibly in the end and forgiving each other. Usually there is even a benefit in the long run because we learn more about each other. I can't be that much of a bully – she is always telling me I am the kindest person she knows – that's why she married me. I just need to remember not to let my own tensions and worries build up, and I need to remind her more just how much I do appreciate her.'
- *Energization*: 'We talked it through after my coaching session and I felt much more in control and back to my usual easy-going self. She laughed at herself for getting so wound up and told me of her plans for taking on a new study course she had been thinking about for years. We also talked about how we would find more time to go out together and get us both out of the work/house routine.'

7 Resolving dilemmas

Many clients come with unresolved dilemmas of various natures. Among the most serious – and interesting – are moral dilemmas where, usually, doing the 'right' thing will involve some potential or actual loss for the client. Some are long-term issues, perhaps involving thoughts of a much-considered career change. Others are more focused on immediate circumstances, perhaps a question about whether to raise a complaint with a boss. Sometimes dilemmas emerge out of the context of other discussions: you can spot these when a client says something like 'Well, on the one hand ...' or 'Well, part of me wants one thing but another part of me wants another....' In these instances the coach can be of service in the first place simply by bringing the dilemma to the full attention of the client. One of the simplest structures for helping your client in this way is the 'name it, claim it, tame it, aim it' approach.

Name it, claim it, tame it and aim it

1. *Name it*: This is about making your client's dilemma explicit. Sometimes dilemmas just seem to float around inside us in the form of rather uncomfortable mixed feelings. For an example of a mixed feeling, remember what it feels like if someone you really care about, with the best of intentions, gives you a strikingly awful present – I have a particular black shirt with red lightning stripes in mind as I write this. Or, perhaps someone you don't really care for very much invites you imploringly to attend a social function: you don't want to go, but you don't want to offend either. Reflect on how these dilemmas can sometimes create feelings of helplessness and disempowerment, perhaps producing hesitant and unconvincing responses. (I never did convince her I liked that shirt, as a matter of fact.) These are of course relatively simple and unimportant examples, unlikely to feature too much in a coaching session, but the principle applies to the bigger dilemmas – unless you explicitly name them, it is hard to deal with them effectively. Naming them brings them directly to your conscious attention in a more coherent form.
2. *Claim it*: This is about taking responsibility for dealing with your dilemma, rather than just letting it drift on. The key is to remind yourself that you have a choice as to how to respond to something

even if it seems that the root cause or blame lies elsewhere. Sometimes it may seem that your dilemma is someone else's doing: but only you can choose to take action on your own behalf. If, on reflection, you decide the dilemma is not really yours alone, you can then decide how to raise it with whoever else is involved.

3. *Tame it*: Some dilemmas can be scary, presenting us with the spectre of loss or of making a big mistake. Sometimes we need to step back and put them in perspective. Useful coaching questions to help with this are:

   • How important is this dilemma on a scale of 0–10 in the context of all the other things that are important in your life?
   • Imagine that two years have passed and you are looking at this dilemma from two years on. How important does it seem now on a 0–10 scale?

   Another way of creating perspective is to create a detached or *disassociated* view of the dilemma. Disassociation is a term used to describe an experience when you are looking at yourself as if from the outside. This can be a very powerful way of reducing the emotional charge of a particular circumstance, allowing you to gain insight and learning. To achieve a disassociated perspective, all you have to do, or ask your client to do, is imagine looking at yourself in the dilemma scenario as if from a distance – say, the other side of the room – and observe yourself 'in action', i.e. as if you were looking at yourself in the dilemma situation. If you get your clients to do this, a useful question to ask them is: 'What do you learn from this perspective?' Very often they will realize they have been making far too much of the dilemma, giving it too much power, and that the answer is in any case rather obvious. There is a direct connection here with the meta-mirror technique. The crux of this is that by looking *at* yourself in the situation that is creating your dilemma, you can create a more detached and less emotionally clouded perspective.

4. *Aim it*: This means resolving to deal with the dilemma and take some positive action, rather than just leaving it to fester. Commitment is the key here. However, the most positive step in *aiming it* is to create in your mind a well-formed outcome for the issue (see Chapter 6 for a description of how to do this).

Richard

Richard was a successful chief executive in the National Health Service. For about six years he had worked in the same Primary Care Trust and had achieved all the goals he had set himself when he had taken on the job. Although he had thought himself content to carry on and consolidate the gains he had made in this post, a new, unexpected job offer was simultaneously exciting and unsettling him. This offer was from a central government department, and in essence offered him a role as a lead consultant advising on a national change programme within the NHS. This offer, exciting and flattering as it was, presented Richard with a number of issues and dilemmas:

- The current job was safe and well known: he had spent years acquiring expertise and experience in this role, and had power, influence and a good reputation, not just within his post but within the local community where he was seen as a leader and 'wise voice' on a number of local issues.
- The new job would be challenging professionally – he was worried that his expertise in managing and leading 'from the front' would be diluted by working in a primarily advisory role, and by the need to acquire a new set of skills in consultancy.
- There were domestic factors: as a family man with young children he would be faced with a great deal of travelling and working away from home at the government headquarters in London, in itself a long commute.
- There was an issue of primary professional identity: by working for the government he could be seen as 'poacher turned gamekeeper' within the health community.

In discussion with Richard he recognized that the issues raised by the new job offer were primarily about his personal and professional *values*: the domestic issues, while important, were secondary in that he felt he was young enough and robust enough to put up with the inconveniences of travel as long as the job itself was right. We agreed that a good use of the coaching sessions we had would be to throw a lot of our time and energy into helping him unravel and understand his core values so that he could make a values-centred decision. We agreed we would try out a particular technique known as 'alter egos' to flush out his core professional values and place them in some kind of order of priority as a basis for making the big decision.

'Alter egos' or 'fantasy figures'

This technique is equally at home in a career change or development context: indeed many client dilemmas are connected with career issues. I learned this technique on my NLP practitioner course in 1988. At that time it was introduced to me as 'fantasy figures' and I coined the term 'alter egos' because it seemed to chime better as a title with our coaching course material. Today it seems almost quaint as an exercise, given its antiquity and absolute simplicity, and yet it continues to bear excellent results as a coaching tool. As with much in coaching, however, simplicity of basic structure needs to be combined with subtlety and sensitivity in practical application for the individual client.

The bare essence of the exercise consists of five carefully worded questions, asked in the following sequence:

1. What is important to you about what you do professionally/for a living?
2. What would you rather be doing professionally/for a living?
3. What is important to you about what you would rather be doing professionally/for a living?
4. Whom do you most admire?
5. What is important to you about this person?

As coach, you would ask your client these questions in sequence, asking them to write down their answers *succinctly*, ideally in a single sentence. However, each question needs to be asked with a degree of explanation. For instance, to the question 'What is important to you about what you do professionally/for a living?', clients sometimes respond with a flippant response of 'Money, of course!' For the occasional client this is literally true – money is their number one motivator – but in my experience most clients, once they have been given the opportunity to think about it in a structured way, recognize that money is not as important as they have sometimes habitually assumed. Clearly it is important to have enough money to meet basic needs, and even enough to feel you are properly valued for your work. But ask your client to consider what is important to them at a deeper level, i.e. what their job represents in terms of what it *means* to them as a person and as a professional. A good prompt can be to ask what their job does for them in terms of *job satisfaction* (but discourage them from including 'job satisfaction' as an answer in itself, because this is a very vague term and means different things to different people: encourage them to be as specific as possible and to write down their answer succinctly – this usually engages them in a few minutes' thought).

For some clients it can be a good idea for you to do the exercise alongside them, to provide them with a model and encourager. I have found in reality that about half my clients enjoy doing the exercise as a shared activity, but it is important to ensure that the spotlight remains firmly on them and that your examples and responses are offered merely as encouragement to be uncensored in their thinking.

In the context of a career review I ran through this exercise with Richard. His answers were as follows:

1. *What is important to you about what you do professionally/for a living?*
    Richard's answer: 'The opportunity to help people grow in terms of
    their ability and confidence, and to work innovatively and col-
    laboratively with a range of talented colleagues – all of this while
    having fun.'

2. *What would you rather be doing professionally/for a living?*
    This apparently simple question can evoke powerful responses. One
    to watch out for is a kind of indignation along the lines of 'How dare
    you imply that there could be any more worthy vocation than
    finance director/hospital manager/civil servant, etc.?' The inference
    that clients can sometimes draw from this particular question is that
    somehow their career is not good enough. Sometimes, incidentally,
    they really *do* think this but do not thank the coach for pointing out,
    however innocently or indirectly, how dissatisfied they have become
    with it: this is potentially a rather spiky area and one where you need
    to choose your words carefully.

    The key here is for the coach to present the question as an
    opportunity for the client to exercise freedom of imagination and to
    let what might be ancient or suppressed desire surface, even if just for
    a moment. The key tone to strike is 'uncensored playfulness'. For the
    more inhibited clients I have at times prompted them to think of
    jobs or careers they hankered after as children, jobs of the engine
    driver variety. For others, another useful prompt is to ask them what
    they would do if money were not an issue, or if they could pursue a
    cherished hobby or interest for a living. It can be important to point
    out that the question does not imply they need to be *actually able or
    capable of fulfilling the job*. You can allow them two or three choices if
    they struggle to settle on one only. Richard's answer to the question
    was: 'Professional sportsman, probably a cricketer or golfer, *or* a
    musician/music producer, playing live on stage and working in the
    studio with rock bands.' Let me assure you, the England cricket
    selectors are unlikely to come knocking on Richard's door, nor are
    the music papers about to clear their front pages in heralding the
    new future of rock'n'roll. The whole point is that Richard allowed
    himself the temporary 'luxury' of thinking about doing something
    just for the hell of it – to let his imagination go and to think without
    inhibition even if only for a short time.

3. *What is important to you about what you would rather be doing pro-
    fessionally/for a living?*
    This is, in general process terms, a repeat of question 1. A useful
    emphasis for both questions is the 'you' – it is important that the
    client feels they do not have to be trying to please anyone else here,
    or somehow justify, perhaps to the coach, their values. Again,

encourage your client to be specific and succinct – one or two sentences should be enough. Here is Richard's answer: 'Being a professional sportsman would allow me to be competitive, physical, be outdoors and would offer adventurous travel. Being a musician/producer would allow me to be collaborative, creative and aesthetically fulfilled, with the bonus of extra adrenalin and a performance kick when playing live.'

4. *Whom do you most admire?*

I have found that I need *plenty* of explanation for this one. Many clients seem reluctant to admit they admire someone fully, so it is best to say that it is all right to have mixed feelings – 'idols have feet of clay' seems to sum it up. At the same time, it is important that clients feel absolutely free to select from the widest possible range: in suggesting a 'no censorship' principle I sometimes make some of the possibilities apparent, emphasizing that the chosen person could be:

- real or fictional
- contemporary or historical
- famous or obscure
- imaginary.

Some clients find it difficult to pick only one person, so I would allow a maximum of three. Richard's chosen three were Gandhi, Spike Milligan and Shane Warne. It is important to recognize that choices on the day represent the *current* values picture or a 'snapshot'.

5. *What is important to you about this person?*

By this point the client is usually well in the groove and needs little prompting to be both specific and succinct. Richard's answers were: 'Gandhi – pursued the highest selfless ideals under extreme pressure while remaining rooted to the material/mundane world without complaint. Milligan – reached for the skies in terms of adventure in humour and remained a dedicated supporter of human rights despite years of debilitating mental illness. Warne – a genuine warrior with a smile, an artist who makes the hardest sporting feats look easy, and an honest, self-deprecating non-conformist.'

Once the client has answered all the questions, the next step is to ask them to mark out the key words, those expressing values or core criteria, in their answers to questions 1, 3 and 5, i.e. the 'What is important .. ?' questions. Simply ask them to underline or circle the words that seem most significant to them. The key step now is to ask the questions that allow them to learn more about their values. Some useful questions are the following:

- How does the overall spread of value words strike you?
- What words (if any) do you notice that stay consistent?

- What changes, if any, do you notice as you look down the list?
- As you look at these words, which now strike you as the most significant?
- What do these value words tell you about the decision you have to make?

Many clients notice that the further down the list they go, the *deeper* the values feel – they tend to attach the most significance to the values that relate to the people they admire. This may be because our 'heroes' are psychologically very important to us – are in fact exemplars of our 'ideal' selves.

I have noticed how the values attached to these heroic figures are often observable in the client themselves. Sometimes it feels useful to draw the client's attention to this, and point out to them that the very quality in someone else they admire is eminently a virtue they themselves possess. This is a coaching technique in its own right, referred to as 'acknowledging': an opportunity to point out to the client a resource state they may have overlooked or simply taken for granted. Despite its simplicity it can have a reinforcing and motivating effect. I remember working with Louise, a hard-working executive from the charity sector: when I pointed out to her just how dedicated and hard-working she was, she seemed to fill with pride and satisfaction – she had begun to take her own commitment for granted and we went on to discuss how perhaps other people in the organization tended to do the same.

Other applications of the 'alter egos' technique

This technique is useful in other situations when a client wants to explore values and meaning in their work or life. For example, some clients express dissatisfaction with their career development, or a fall-off in job satisfaction, and 'alter egos' can be a great way for them to explore what seems to be missing. In these circumstances there are some other very useful questions, such as the following:

- How could you get more of what is important to you in what you are currently doing?
- In what other ways might you seek to have these values met, either inside or outside your working life?
- What would you have to change in your circumstances for you to get more of what is important to you?

After many years of using this exercise I have consistently found it to be a reliable way of approaching an apparently heavy subject – values – in a palatable, light and even fun way. Nonetheless clients consistently extract the necessary depth from this analysis of their values: many clients describe it as an emotionally moving experience. Some clients say they have not been asked to think about their values in anything but a very superficial way since the day they started work – strange, when you think about how important our values are to our motivation and performance, and how much many organizations talk about 'valuing' their employees.

The 'peak experience' technique

This technique is useful in a number of coaching circumstances. Even just as an energy-raiser for a client who has got a bit stuck or bogged down in an issue, it has great value. However, as with the 'alter egos' technique, it can also have huge value in helping clients to resolve dilemmas by helping them to get clarity on what is really important to them. It is very much an exercise that works on the 'being' self or that part of the self involving identity, values and beliefs, although it is a relatively lighthearted and enjoyable experience for the client – indeed this is why it works, enabling a client to do deep work without burdening them with onerous language or structure.

The core of the technique is about helping a client to identify when they were at their essential best in any context of life – some people refer to being in 'flow' – and to help them to realize consciously what factors were particularly important to them at these 'peak' moments. This knowledge can then feed into their decision-making about particular dilemmas or 'big issues' they might be facing.

Tony was a senior civil servant who was facing up to the fact that his career seemed to have lost some of its sparkle – he simply wasn't experiencing the level of satisfaction he had previously had, but was not sure why this was happening. He had reached a point where he was in a dilemma – should he pack in his civil service career and look for something else? And if he were to do this, what would it be?

I introduced the idea of the peak experience exercise and asked Tony to talk about one or more times when he felt absolutely at his best – when his senses were heightened, when he felt deeply and joyously engaged. I explained to him that while he spoke to me about each of these experiences I would write down every word that seemed to have a bearing or influence on his experience. Tony spoke enthusiastically about how he had organized his recent 40th birthday party, one of those 'big' birthdays when clients are often engaged in soul-searching about their careers. As he spoke his eyes seemed to light up: he went into tremendous detail about the great care he had lavished on the preparations and how much he had enjoyed being the host of what indeed seemed a glittering occasion.

At the end of his account of the great night I had two pages of key words and short phrases scrawled down. I asked Tony to look at these and pick ten that seemed to him to have particular resonance with the quality of the occasion. I then asked him to narrow his choice down to the top three words or phrases – words that for him summed up the absolute essence of the night. His three chosen words were:

- friendship
- caring/hospitality
- showing off!

We went on to discuss the significance of these words to him and his career, and he reflected on how little of any of these things he was currently experiencing at work. We went on to discuss the actions he would need to take to get more of these things in his work – he was able to identify a number of actions he could pursue to this end fairly quickly. He left the session excited to have identified real steps he could take to get more of these x factors back into his career. What had been building in his mind as a potentially drastic turning point resolved itself into a succinct and focused action plan based on what was really important to him in terms of operating at his very best.

Summary of the peak experience technique

Explain to your client what you mean by peak experience. Some people refer to it as being 'in flow' or being 'in the zone' – a term likely to find resonance with sporty people in particular. You might offer some typical factors often present in peak moments, such as the following:

- losing awareness of time
- a sense of effortless ease
- feeling confident, assured of success
- a sense of joyousness even in a serious activity
- using all or some of your learned and innate abilities.

Get your client to describe one, two or even three of these experiences from *any* context of their life. For each one, go through the process of writing down all the key words and phrases, and then narrowing these down with your client to the top few. You can then take your client through a review of how the way forward through their current dilemma can be informed by their insights into 'them at their best'.

Here is a worked example of the 'peak experience' technique taken from one of our coaching course demonstrations: this involved a coaching tutor running through the technique with a student while someone else from the learning group wrote down all the key words on a flipchart.

Elaine's peak experience flipchart looked like this (with the first choice of key words *italicized* and the final selection of key words ***italicized* in bold**)

Experience 1: doing a stand-up comedy routine
Business school; uproot and move on; lived and breathed; socializing; stand-up *comedy*; ***standing in front of my peers***; enjoyed the effect it had on audience; *funny* story; adrenalin; ***going out on a limb***; labelled as feminist; people rolling in the aisles; holding court with humour; funny; light teasing way; brisk; nerve-wracking; my role is to shake it up; 75% conservative men; not rocking people but pushing them to slightly altered state; laughter; 200 people; microphone; relief after done; 'that was amazing what you did'; ***appropriate but pushing it a bit***

Experience 2: a day out with my children
Hever Castle; autumn with children, youngest two years running down the hill; in the 'mum-zone'; ***serenity***; ***energy***; ***excitement***; provided that for my children; 'clucky'; I can do this, this works sometimes; a lightness; said out loud 'Do you notice how nice this is?'; captured the moment for mum; I had got us there; ***taken by surprise***; ***feeling it emerged***; there was this feeling; ***unplanned***

Elaine clearly enjoyed revisiting these special moments in her life, and afterwards was particularly engaged in talking about the parts of the experience that had included surprise, things emerging and being unplanned, and how she might look to create opportunities for more of that kind of experience in her work.

Parts negotiation

An NLP classic, this exercise encapsulates many of the principles and pre-suppositions of both coaching and NLP. Of all the dilemma resolution exercises, this is the one that can get to the heart of the kind of dilemma where your client says something like 'Well, part of me really wants to do *x*, but another part of me really wants to do *y*.' The vast majority of these dilemmas revolve around the dimensions of safety ↔ security, known ↔ unknown, or familiarity ↔ adventure, but be prepared to encounter other kinds of dilemma too. When the dilemma is about a really important change, the client can describe feeling torn or twisted apart, wracked or tormented by opposing urges.

The exercise begins the process of resolving the dilemma in a way that actively promotes internal congruence. In this exercise every 'part' of the self engaged in the dilemma receives conscious acknowledgement and respect, even those parts of the self that are acting, or feeling, awkward or difficult. This is a very important aspect of the exercise, because it gets completely away from the idea that 'part' of you is in the wrong, or being weak. It therefore conforms fully to the presupposition that 'every behaviour has a positive intention', one of the very core principles in NLP. No part of the self is demonized or ridiculed.

A potential obstacle to this exercise is that for some clients it might seem somewhat 'way out' or 'New Age'. It is an exercise that should be introduced with due attention to the client's prevailing world view, in the interests of rapport and of serving *only* the client's agenda. I remember vividly a wildly angry potential client who had come to talk about the possibility of being coached by me saying, as almost her first words, 'If you mention the word "spiritual" to me I might punch you in the face!' This would not be the first exercise you would introduce to a client of this frame of mind.

Richard

Richard was the NHS chief executive I went through the 'alter egos' exercise with. He was wrestling with taking on a job that would require him to travel and act in a consultancy rather than an executive role. The alter ego exercise was enough to give him a good work-through of some of the values he wanted to have expressed in his work, but his essential dilemma, whether to change jobs, was not resolved. In his case his dilemma was expressed in its essence as 'Part of me wants to stay where I am, doing what I know, and another part of me wants to try the new role and step into a wider sphere.' He agreed to try the parts negotiation technique.

The parts negotiation technique

- Ask your client to name the dilemma they face, in a sentence that goes 'Part of me wants *a*, while another part of me wants *b*.' Let the client know you are going to set up a conversation between these parts.
- Ask the client to go inside themselves (they may wish to close their eyes) and identify the part of themselves that wants *a*. Encourage them to identify the specific location inside themselves where this part resides – clients virtually always have an instinctive feel for this, but if they do not, ask them to identify where the part would be if they *did* know where it was – they will get it in the end. Keep the tone positive and cheerful, and work on the assumption that the

questions make sense to the client and will elicit the needed response – in short, be confident yourself so that the client will feel confident.

- Ask them to identify what the part that wants *a* looks like, sounds like and feels like. You will need to be prepared for virtually anything – clients have variously reported to me that the 'part' is a little person, a colour, one of a variety of abstract shapes, cartoon faces, or just a particular feeling or sound. Suggest they say 'hello' to the part, and establish some rapport with it: again, some clients may think this a little odd at first, and if necessary repeat for them that the exercise is based on the establishment of internal rapport.

- Ask your client to ask this part what it is *trying* to do *for* them – what its positive intention is. Get them to listen to the response the part gives and then thank the part for what it is *intending* to do on their behalf.

- Get your client to ask the part that wants *a* what it thinks about the part that wants *b*. Acknowledge its opinion, and let it know you will be back to talk to it in a while.

- Repeat all the above for the part that wants *b*.

- Get your client to ask further questions to each part about what each is *fundamentally* trying to do on their behalf. For each answer offered by each part – often it is something very fundamental like growth, security or happiness – get the client to ask what *that* is trying to do. Ultimately both the parts will recognize they are looking for some of the same things for your client – they have interests in common.

- Get your client to ask each part in turn if they are willing to talk together to find a way forward on the dilemma – the 'parts' may initially be reluctant, and if so, get your client to reassure them that they (the client) respect both parts fully and will be impartial.

- Get the client to ask each part where it would feel comfortable to have a conversation about the dilemma.

- Get your client to have the parts meet together inside. Their job is going to be to have a discussion about the dilemma with a view to finding a way forward.

- In the interests of internal ecology, get your client to check round inside themselves for any other 'part' that may object to the meeting – this has never happened in my experience but it reassures the client that you are thinking about their whole wellbeing.

- Get your client to leave the parts alone for a time, while reassuring them they (the client) will be back to check out their answer in a given time – perhaps an hour, or a day – whatever the client thinks is suitable.

- Hold your client accountable for meeting the appointment. They will need to go back inside and find out what the two parts have come up with.

Richard's 'parts' were interesting and full of character: he represented the internal conflict as something like a medieval court drama. The part that wanted Richard to stay where he was, was represented as the king of the court. As the master of the domain he was happy with his power and with the familiarity of his realm, and was worried at the prospect of losing his unquestioned authority. But he also felt a little constrained by the metaphorical gates of the kingdom.

The part that wanted to move on was a kind of court wizard, a Merlin figure who firmly wanted adventure outside the gates of the kingdom and who was keen to test out his knowledge and his skills in other lands: formal authority was less of an issue for him because he felt his personal power to be invested in his skills and knowledge.

Each part was initially somewhat sceptical of the other, but they discovered through the process of internal conversation that both had in common a wish for success for Richard, an important part of which was a desire for high professional status. In this particular instance money played an important part because the higher salary on offer in Richard's potential new job represented success and status to both parts – this was the common ground. He resolved to take the new job.

Variations

There are numerous ways of tweaking the technique. For example, if the client reports that the 'parts' seem unsure how to get into a conversation, or are stuck for ideas, you can suggest contacting another internal 'part', perhaps a wise or creative part, whose job it is to 'facilitate' the internal process: sometimes clients have achieved very specific results when I have suggested they set the 'facilitator' part a set task, such as getting the other two parts to agree, say, three ideas for the way forward in the agreed time. The core principles of seeking internal rapport and congruence are exactly the same as the parts negotiation exercise, as is much of the technique.

Julie

Julie was a young marketing specialist working for a small but successful media company, whose issue was not so much a dilemma as a reluctance to engage in the very necessary task of organizing herself domestically – a surprisingly common issue among successful career-people. Julie simply did not like doing any housework at all and was only prepared to pay for a limited amount of domestic help, which meant she still lived in too much mess. As we discussed the issue, it began to express itself as a classic parts division: 'Part of me really wants to get organized but another part of me just wants to chill out and relax when I'm at home.'

We went through the stages of contacting the two parts. Julie saw her 'wants to be organized' part as something of a 'goody-goody' in the domestic context, dressed as a school prefect and with a rather stern expression. Her 'just want to chill out' part was by contrast a wild punk rocker – leather jacket, Doc Marten boots and dyed hair. Not surprisingly, the two parts were not getting on that well over that particular issue. We called in the services of a third internal part we called her creative part. 'He' (internal parts seem to be interchangeable in terms of gender) was given the job of coming up with three different ways that would meet the needs of both the other parts.

In fact, he only needed one idea to come up with a solution with which both Julie's other internal parts were happy. This was for her to do housework to loud rock music: this way the 'punk' part was happy she was having fun and the 'prefect' was pleased to get the place tidied up.

Another variation, or even addition, to the technique is to bring in a physical dimension, using the metaphor of 'on the one hand' and 'on the other hand' in an explicitly physical way. Get the client to locate the two conflicting positions (e.g. 'security' versus 'adventure' in the hands them-selves, so that each hand physically represents one of the parts. Get the client to hold their hands in front of them, and ask each hand/part what their positive intention is. Get the client to continue asking probing questions about these positive intentions until they find out the common ground, i.e. what the parts are both ultimately trying to achieve, for example a high-level outcome such as 'happiness'. Get the client to imagine the 'security' and the 'adventure' (for example) hands coming together to create a new combined or 'super' part representing 'happiness'. Finally, get the client to bring their hands towards their chest and symbolically 'integrate' the new super part, leaving it to do its work.

The fine detail of technique is easy to manage if the following principles are kept to:

- Remember that every behaviour has a positive intention.
- Take the trouble to create rapport at all points – internal rapport is as important as external rapport.
- Ecological solutions are the only ones that stick, so make sure that whatever comes out of the exercise chimes well with the whole person and the system they live in.
- Allow a little playfulness and use language that suggests the client will be able to do the visualization quite easily.

Time-line work

The way we think about time and represent it to ourselves through our senses varies enormously from person to person. I remember how shocked I was when I first learned this – I had never really thought about it, and had assumed that the way we managed time in our heads was much the same for all of us, except perhaps for the fact that we placed different values on punctuality. However, working with other students on a course helped me to realize that we represent time in hugely different ways. What is more, the *way* in which we represent time has a big impact on how we manage ourselves and think about ourselves, including how we respond to dilemmas.

We manage concepts of past and future in distinct ways. For some of us, the future is a picture some distance in front of us, for others it may be a picture placed to our left or right. Similarly the past may be represented as literally behind us or to our right or left. The visual variations are many in terms of distance, size, colour and clarity of picture, to name but a few possibilities. Our emotional responses to these pictures of past and future vary enormously too.

Try answering these questions for yourself:

- Picture a pleasant memory from yesterday. Where is it in relation to you? Close by? Distant? Behind you or to the side?
- Ditto a pleasant memory from six months ago.
- Ditto ten years ago.
- Ditto from early childhood.
- Picture something you are anticipating with pleasure tomorrow. Where is this image in relation to you? Close by? Distant? In front of you or to the side?
- Ditto something pleasant a few months in the future.
- Ditto something several years in the future.

You might like to draw out the shape of your personal time-line on paper. I sometimes get clients to take a piece of paper and draw a small picture of the top of their head in the middle (nose pointing north), and then get them to answer the questions above and mark out on the paper the points where they picture the past and future, using an approximate scale of measurement. They can then 'join the dots' to get a general idea of how their personal line shapes up. It can take practice to establish the patterns by which you personally order and represent time. Most people seem to have either a front/back system (in which the future is in front and the past behind), or a left/right system (in which the past is usually to the left and the future to the right). Some clients will see a year away in the future or the past as being literally miles away from them, while others might picture it as being just a few metres away or less: the degree of variation from person to person really is striking.

Occasionally a client will simply not relate to the whole concept of time having a recognizable spatial element for them, perhaps instead asserting that all their memories and thoughts about the future are in the same place, inside their head. I have not generally found it useful to persist down this line of enquiry when the client is at all reluctant, because it may be that they have an intellectual resistance to something they regard as unorthodox. Maintaining rapport and the confidence of the client is almost always more important than insisting upon a particular technique. However, the majority of clients will begin to quickly recognize at least some of the main ways in which they work with, or represent, time. At the very least we as coaches need to recognize that we will all have a different relationship to time, and should not assume that how we organize time ourselves is likely to be shared by our clients.

Sometimes our language can suggest a lot about the ways in which we habitually relate to time, when we use phrases such as:

- looking *forward* to something
- putting something *behind* you
- looking a long way *ahead*
- leaving issues *to one side*.

Sometimes a client will offer you big clues as to how they are managing their relationship to time when they use their hands to illustrate what they are saying, for example by gesturing over their shoulder when talking about the past or by waving a hand to the right or left when talking about past or future.

Practical applications of the time-line

Sometimes when a client seems stuck or is wrestling with a dilemma, time, or their perception of it as it applies to them, is the hidden cause of the issue. Typically this involves how they think about the future: for example, when the 'near' future seems to them to be miles away, this may explain why they do not seem motivated to do any planning or take any action to prepare for it.

Susan

Susan was a trainer working in management development. Her career was developing somewhat slowly in her estimation, but she was not really sure why. It emerged that she had never really planned for the future, but tended just to live on a day-by-day basis, and she had begun to notice a degree of dissatisfaction with this. Her expressed dilemma was what to do next in developing her career. I introduced the idea of time-lines to her because I had a hunch that her lack of planning and dynamism in developing her career might in part at least be related to her perception of herself in relation to time. Susan found the idea fascinating, and we went through an exercise using the questions outlined above in which she plotted out her own time-line, past and future. The results of this were a revelation to her. It seemed her 'past' time-line appeared as a steep curve behind her. This gave her the worrying sensation that she was 'falling' from her past, and this falling sensation gave her the feeling that she could not really exercise control over her life and career. At the same time her future line seemed to stretch miles ahead of her, to the point that anything more than a few weeks seemed an irrelevant distance ahead and not really worth thinking about in detail or with any urgency. We discussed what would be a more helpful representation of time, and in the end I asked her to imagine two important adjustments to her time-line. First, I suggested to Susan that she imagine her 'past' line levelling out behind her, and when she did this she said it made her feel less anxious about the past and much more in control of her life. Next I asked her to imagine that her future was literally moving towards her, in the sense of getting physically nearer. Susan found this quite an emotionally moving experience, recognizing that her future was in fact directly 'within her grasp' (her words). She seemed hugely relieved that she was able to exercise far more control over both her feelings about the past and her ability to plan for the future. We went on to discuss her career direction dilemmas with a far greater sense of energy and focus on her part.

This example is just about raising awareness of time-lines with your clients and giving them a sense of choice and control over their personal experience of time. Other issues involving time-lines can be more complex and emotionally charged, particularly where unhappy memories are concerned. For much greater depth on this subject I would recommend you read *Time Line Therapy and the Basis of Personality* by Tad James and Wyatt Woodsmall (1989). This book explains many far more sophisticated techniques involving time-lines, including some 'quick therapy' techniques that involve moving back through your time-line to discover the original source of an anxiety or fear in order to do some 're-scripting' of your experience. There is also some interesting exploration of cultural dimensions of time, and some ideas connected to reincarnation that may challenge or irritate.

8 End note

On the subject of time, you have to make coaching choices right in the moment

Ultimately the choice of technique, or variation within it, at any given moment, is a judgement call for the coach. This is true of all coaching scenarios, and is what makes coaching something that cannot be learned purely from books, because it is something live, dynamic and immediate. Coaches need to learn to work in the reality of the moment, with most of their attention focused directly on the client, not in the realms of theory. The finest learning environment for coaching is the coaching room itself. This does not mean your clients are merely guinea pigs on which you test out your skills and techniques, but it does mean you will only come to develop your judgement of what to do, and when to do it, from lengthy practice. Every moment of every session involves choice for the coach in terms of how you behave: these choices need to be weighed up against many factors, including client behaviour, mood and energy, the quality of rapport, the aims of the session, self-management issues, time factors, raw instinct, and a host of other variables that are in constant flux and motion. Only coaching in the flesh and in the moment can aid you in the development of your confidence and sureness of touch; but as these surely grow in your own coaching, hopefully the ideas in this book will add to the filters though which you reach your coaching decisions and add a little more to your repertoire of choice.

Bibliography

Bandler, R. and Grinder, J. (1979) *Frogs into Princes*, Moab, UT: Real People Press.

Bentley, T. (2002) *A Touch of Magic*, Gloucestershire: The Space Between Publishing.

Csikszentmihalyi, M. and Csikszentmihalyi, I. (1988) *Optimal Experience*, Cambridge University Press.

Dilts, R. (1996) *Visionary Leadership Skills*, Capitola, CA: Meta Publications.

Gallwey, W.T., (1986) *The Inner Game of Tennis*, London: Pan Macmillan.

Gilpin, A. (1998) *Unstoppable People*, London: Random House.

Goleman, G. (1996) *Emotional Intelligence*, London: Bloomsbury.

Havens, R.A. (1985) *The Wisdom of Milton H. Erickson*, New York Irvington.

James, T. and Woodsmall, W. (1989) *Time Line Therapy and the Basis of Personality*, Capitola, CA: Meta Publications.

Jeffers, S. (1997) *Feel the Fear and Do It Anyway*, London: Rider.

Knight, S. (1995) *NLP at Work*, London: Nicholas Brealey.

Lakoff, G. and Johnson, M. (1981) *Metaphors We Live By*, University of Chicago Press.

McDermott, I. and Jago, W. (2001) *The NLP Coach*, London: Piatkus.

McKenna, P. (2006) *Instant Confidence*, London: Bantam.

Morgan, G. (1997) *Images of Organization*, Thousand Oaks, CA: SAGE.

O'Connor, J. and Lages, A. (2004) *Coaching with NLP*, London: Element.

O'Connor, J. and Seymour, J. (1994) *Training with NLP*, London: Thorsons.

Rogers, C.R. (1951) *Client Centred Therapy*, Boston, MA: Houghton Mifflin.

Rogers, J. (2004) *Coaching Skills: A Handbook*, Maidenhead: Open University Press.

Seligman, M. (2003) *Authentic Happiness*, London: Nicholas Brealey.

Index

Page numbers in *italics* refer to figures